# PLAY NOW.

# THRIVE LATER.

**The Brain Well-Being Model® and**

**Collective Care in Action®**

*A Framework for Healing
Individuals, Families, and Communities*

**Nakeya T. Fields, LCSW, PPSC, Registered
Play Therapist-Supervisor**

**Foreword by: Ruby Guillen, MSW, CIS**

**The Therapeutic Play Foundation, Inc.**

**Los Angeles, California**

*First edition, March 2026*

*Brain Well-Being Model® is a registered trademark of Nakeya Fields, Licensed Clinical Social Worker PC. Collective Care in Action®, Resilience Studio™, and associated frameworks are trademarks and proprietary intellectual property of the author.*

*This book is intended for educational purposes only and is not a substitute for medical, psychological, or mental health treatment. Readers seeking clinical care should consult a licensed professional.*

*ISBN 978-1-948568-07-4 (hardcover)*
*ISBN 978-1-948568-05-0 (paperback)*
*ISBN 978-1-948568-06-7 (ebook)*

*Library of Congress Control Number: 2026904195*

*Published by The Therapeutic Play Foundation, Inc.*
*Los Angeles, California*

*playnowthrivelater.com*

# Dedication

**For my son, Amare**, whose curiosity, laughter, and becoming remind me every day that healing must always leave room for joy.

**For Nova and Oreo**, faithful companions in quiet moments of reflection and gentle teachers of presence.

**For my family**, whose love made survival possible and whose strength made purpose inevitable.

**For the team members, colleagues, and quiet builders** who gave energy, labor, ideas, patience, and heart to work that often asked more than it returned.

If you carried any part of the effort, you helped shape the outcome.

And for every child, parent, healer, educator, and community leader still learning how to rest, reconnect, and begin again, may this work make room for your healing too.

# Acknowledgments

This work was never created alone.

It grew from relationships, from communities, and from the many places where people continue to practice care, healing, and play together.

I am deeply grateful to the mentors, teachers, colleagues, and cultural healers whose wisdom lives within these pages.

To the clinicians, educators, community health workers, doulas, faith leaders, artists, gardeners, and youth wellness leaders who continue to show that healing is relational, embodied, and shared, thank you for carrying this work forward in everyday spaces of life.

— — — —

I am especially grateful to *Kyla Eveillard of Naza Locs* in Los Angeles for generously sharing her Social Story Window. Her work reminds us that healing often lives in everyday community spaces—in the chair, in conversation, and in the care people offer one another.

Special thanks to *Chelle Jones* for her creative partnership and graphic design work on the cover of this book. Beyond her design talent, Chelle has been a thoughtful collaborator as new ideas emerged and took shape along the way. I deeply appreciate the care and creativity she brought to this process. Her support helped make **Play Now. Thrive Later.** a reality.

I also want to thank *Jodi Smith, Registered Play Therapist Supervisor, RPT-S™*, for introducing me to the transformative power of play and guiding me into this important work. Her mentorship helped shape the path that led to this book.

To my trusted colleague in education, *Dr. Freda Rossi*, thank you for seeing and trusting the fullness of who I am, and for walking alongside me in bringing Compassionate Systems of Awareness into spaces where healing and growth can take root.

— — —

I offer special gratitude to the therapeutic and scholarly lineages that informed this work, including attachment research, polyvagal theory, public health equity movements, and Gestalt-based play therapy.

As a Gestalt-based play therapist, I hold deep appreciation for the work of Violet Oaklander, whose teachings on presence, relationship, and the healing power of play profoundly shaped my professional journey. Her work continues to inspire my commitment to expanding the conversation about healing toward collective care.

— — —

To my family and ancestors, whose resilience made my work possible.

To my child, who reminds me each day that joy is both medicine and direction.

— — —

And to every reader who carries a quiet hope that healing—personal and collective—is still possible: this book is for you.

May these pages offer permission to play, to reconnect, and to imagine new ways of caring for ourselves and one another.

# Epigraph

Healing is not only the absence of harm.

It is the presence of connection,

the freedom to play,

and the courage to thrive together.


— Nakeya T. Fields

# The Brain Well-Being Model®

The Brain Well-Being Model® describes four interconnected forms of awareness—somatic, perceptual, relational, and aspirational—that help individuals recognize what is happening within and around them. Together, these pathways support movement from protective states toward healing, connection, and purposeful growth.

Awareness creates options. Options support regulation, healing, and choice.

# Moving Through the Mode States

Human functioning is dynamic. We move through Guard, Healing, and Thrive in response to stress, safety, memory, environment, and relationship. The goal is not to remain in one mode, but to develop awareness of what each state requires so that movement becomes more intentional, flexible, and supportive of well-being.

Modes are responsive states, not fixed identities.

Mobility, not perfection.

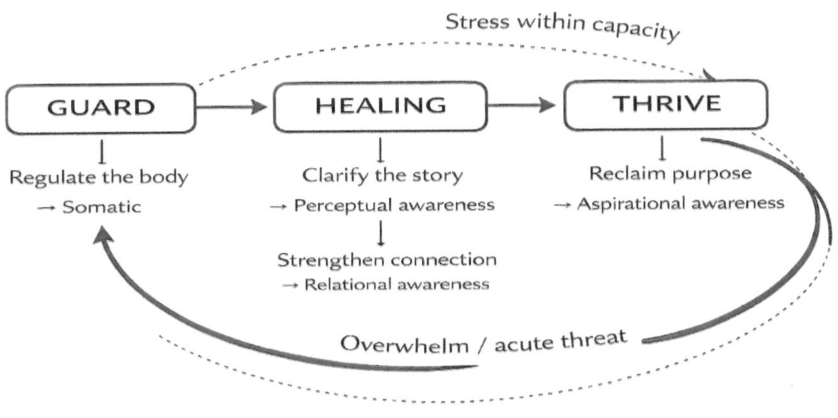

# *Foreword*

**by Ruby Guillen, MSW, CIS**

Across continents and communities, people are searching for language to describe a shared human experience: the feeling of living in prolonged uncertainty while still longing for connection, dignity, and peace. This book arrives at a critical moment in that search.

My own work has been shaped in the spaces where systems meet human crisis, responding to severe child abuse and family violence, sitting with data that should never have had to exist, and listening to families and communities who carry the impact long after the headlines fade. In national and global advocacy spaces, I have seen social workers, public health professionals, technologists, and youth leaders come together with one shared conviction: our responses to harm must become more humane, more preventative, and more rooted in the wisdom of communities. Again and again, the same question surfaces: how do we build systems that protect life instead of simply documenting loss?

In that context, *Play Now. Thrive Later.* is not simply another contribution to mental health literature. It is a map for the world that children, families, and frontline workers have been asking for, a world where we do not wait for crisis before we care and where healing is understood as a collective responsibility rather than an individual task.

Drawing from neuroscience, public health, trauma studies, education, and community based healing traditions, Nakeya T. Fields offers more than a clinical model. She offers a relational vision of well-being, one that recognizes that the nervous system is shaped not only by what happens inside a therapy room but also by history, environment, culture, and everyday relationship.

The Brain Well-Being Model® and Collective Care in Action® invite us to design environments in which regulation, belonging, and hope are not rare outcomes but expected conditions of daily life. They give shared language to what community health workers, social workers, and local healers have long practiced, often without formal recognition, that healing is relational, embodied, and collective.

What makes this work especially powerful is that it does not live only in theory. It is grounded in lived community practice in schools and families, faith spaces and neighborhood programs, barbershops and salons, community gardens and youth-led initiatives, particularly within Black communities in Los Angeles. For those of us who work with both the data and the people behind it, these examples feel both urgent and profoundly hopeful. They show that prevention is not abstract. It looks like real people creating real spaces of safety, play, and connection.

This book also speaks into the growing global conversation about how technology, data, and policy can either deepen harm or support healing. The Brain Well-Being Index and the language of Guard Mode, Healing Mode, and Thrive Mode offer more than clinical tools. They offer a humane lens we can carry into our decisions about systems, platforms, and resources.

At its heart, this book poses a simple yet transformative question: what becomes possible when healing is organized around connection instead of crisis? The pages that follow do not offer easy answers. Instead, they offer something more durable, a usable framework for compassionate systems capable of supporting humans thriving across generations through individual practice, community care, and structural change. As someone who has witnessed both the fragility and the courage of the human nervous system, I see in this work a pathway toward the kind of world our children deserve.

Ruby Guillen, MSW, CIS

CEO, Humanistic Technologies

Senior technologist and research analyst in fatal and severe child abuse and family violence, 2026

# CONTENTS

# When Healing Becomes Collective Knowledge

There has never been a time in human history when so many people were exposed to so much information, uncertainty, and unprocessed stress at the same time. Across communities, the same quiet questions continue to surface. Why does my body stay tense even when nothing is wrong? Why is rest so difficult to trust? Why does hope feel fragile instead of natural? Most importantly, what actually helps people heal?

For decades, answers to these questions were scattered across different scientific and cultural traditions, including neuroscience, trauma psychology, attachment research, public health, somatic therapies, play therapy, cultural healing practices, and community care movements. Each field carried part of the truth. Very few spaces brought these insights together in a way that families, educators, clinicians, and communities could use in everyday life. This book was written to become that bridge.

# A Shift in Perspective

Traditional mental health systems often position healing as an individual clinical task, something that happens inside an office between a provider and a patient after harm has already occurred. Biology, history, and community experience tell a different story. Healing is not only clinical. It is relational, cultural, environmental, and collective.

When stress becomes chronic through trauma, racism, poverty, displacement, community violence, or historical inequity, the nervous system adapts for survival. This protective adaptation is not failure. It is intelligence. In this book, that adaptive survival state is called Guard Mode. Guard Mode protects life. However, when protection lasts too long, it begins to limit connection, learning, health, imagination, and possibility.

The question is not how to eliminate Guard Mode. The deeper question is how to help the brain and body remember that safety, joy, and connection are still possible.

## The Three Integrated Contributions of This Work

This text introduces three interconnected frameworks designed to answer that question in both theory and practice.

## 1. The Brain Well-Being Model®

A neuroscience informed structure describing four domains of awareness: somatic, perceptual, relational, and aspirational. These domains explain how humans move from survival toward regulation, healing, and thriving.

**2. Collective Care in Action®**

A real world implementation pathway demonstrating that healing occurs through relationships, community environments, shared responsibility, and culturally responsive systems rather than isolation.

**3. Play Now. Thrive Later.**

A practical philosophy grounded in play therapy, creative expression, nature connection, somatic regulation, and culturally intelligent care. It shows that resilience develops through lived experience, not insight alone.

Together, these three structures form a usable system for clinicians, educators, community health workers, faith leaders, families, youth, and future healers. You do not need clinical training to understand this work. You only need curiosity about healing.

## Origins in Compassionate Systems

The early architecture of this model was influenced by exposure to Compassionate Systems of Awareness within educational leadership environments. These were spaces where administrators were being trained to understand nervous system regulation, trauma impact, and relational safety even when clinical professionals were not present. That exposure revealed something important. Mental well being knowledge was beginning to reach systems of power, but it had not yet reached everyday community life.

This book continues that translation. It moves ideas from theory to practice, from systems to families, and from insight to lived healing.

## An Invitation to the Reader

This is not a book meant only to be read. It is meant to be used. As you move through these pages, you are invited to notice your body, your relationships, your memories of safety, and your access to joy. Pause when something feels familiar. Return to restorative practices when needed.

If this book succeeds in its purpose, you will leave with something both simple and powerful: a new way to understand healing and a clear path to begin practicing it in everyday life.

# How to Use This Book

This book was written to be lived with, not just read once and shelved. Different readers will enter it from different doors. Parents, caregivers, community health workers, clinicians, educators, youth leaders, system builders, policy makers, and people simply trying to survive in a world that feels too heavy may all find their way here. You do not need a mental health degree to use what is in these pages. You only need a nervous system and a willingness to care.

## Moving Through the Parts

The chapters are organized in an intentional arc.

Part I names Guard Mode and traces how stress, trauma, and history shape the nervous system. It gives language to experiences many people have carried without words.

Part II introduces the Brain Well-Being Model® and the four awareness domains, somatic, perceptual, relational, and aspirational, as a shared map.

Part III looks at where healing is already happening in everyday life and how to design enriched environments that support regulation and connection.

Part IV turns toward systems, workforce, and policy, asking how the model can live inside clinics, schools, plans, and community organizations.

Part V gathers the threads into a wider lens on collective thriving, play, and the world we are building for the next generation.

You can read straight through or move through the book based on your needs. If you are new to this language, beginning at the start will help the later chapters land more gently. If you are a practitioner or leader looking for implementation ideas, you may find yourself returning most often to Parts III through V and the appendices, circling back to earlier chapters when grounding is helpful.

## If You Are Reading As

Some readers will approach this book from specific roles or responsibilities.

Parents, caregivers, or family members may spend more time with the early chapters on Guard Mode, the personal and intergenerational stories, and the practical sections in Parts III and V. The appendices on Seeds and Leaves, F.L.O.W.S., and everyday collective care offer simple practices that can be adapted at home.

Community health workers, peer supporters, educators, or youth leaders may find the Brain Well-Being Model®, the Guard, Healing, and Thrive language, and the examples of community spaces in Parts III and IV to be their core tools. The Brain Well-Being Index appendices in B and C, along with the practice guides in D through F, can support reflection, group work, and conversations without requiring clinical training.

Clinicians, supervisors, or organizational leaders may find the full arc of the book relevant, from individual nervous system states to broader systems change. Pay particular attention to how

Guard Mode appears in both bodies and institutions, and how Brain Well-Being Index data is meant to support, not replace, professional judgment. Appendix G offers starting points for implementation and partnership.

Systems leaders, policy makers, and funder partners may move more quickly through Parts I and II and spend more time in Parts IV and V, as well as Appendix G, where workforce development, CalAIM style efforts, measurement, and infrastructure are discussed. The question here may be less "Is this true?" and more "What would it mean to invest in this way of understanding care?"

## Trauma Informed Reading

Some stories and examples in this book touch on trauma, racism, and loss. You are not expected to read through discomfort without pause. You can take breaks, skip sections and return later, read with others so connection is available when material feels close to home, and notice your own Guard, Healing, or Thrive state as you move through the pages.

You are always allowed to choose what is right for your body at this moment. That choice is part of the work.

## Using the Appendices and Tools

The appendices are designed as practice companions.

Appendix A provides a technical overview of the Brain Well-Being Index™.

Appendices B and C offer guidelines for Brain Well-Being Index administration, scoring, interpretation, and clinical integration.

Appendices D through F translate the model into concrete practices, including Seeds and Leaves, F.L.O.W.S., and everyday collective care rhythms.

Appendix G speaks directly to implementation and partnership.

You do not need to use every tool. Begin with one or two practices that feel doable and relevant, then adapt them to your culture and setting. The goal is not to replicate a script but to protect the core values: dignity before data, safety before insight, context before interpretation, and support before separation.

## A Final Orientation

This book is not asking you to carry everything alone. It invites you into a shared language and a shared project, helping more bodies, families, communities, and systems spend less time in Guard Mode and more time in Healing and Thrive. Take what serves your context, leave what does not, and, whenever possible, practice in community. The work of collective care was never meant to be done in isolation.

# Chapter 1

# Why the Brain Learns Survival First

Before the brain learns language, before it learns mathematics, and before it learns rules about who it is allowed to become, the brain learns one essential question: Am I safe?

This question is older than memory, older than culture, and older than words. It lives in the nervous system, the biological network constantly scanning for danger or protection. Every sound, facial expression, tone of voice, and movement becomes data.

## How the Body Answers "Am I Safe?"

The nervous system does not wait for conscious thought to make this decision. It reads subtle cues such as eye contact, muscle tension, sounds in the room, the rhythm of a caregiver's voice, and many other signals from the surrounding environment. Based on these cues, the body shifts into different states. When signals of safety are present, the system supports connection, curiosity, and social engagement. When cues of threat appear, the body prepares for fight, flight, or shutdown, often before a person is aware that anything has changed.

This means behavior is not random. It is the body's best attempt to answer that ancient question in real time: Am I safe?

When safety is consistent, the nervous system opens. Curiosity grows. Connection feels natural. Learning becomes joyful.

When safety is unpredictable, the nervous system protects instead. Attention narrows. Energy shifts toward vigilance. The body prepares for danger whether danger is present or not.

This is not a disorder. It is adaptation. The brain is doing exactly what it was designed to do: keep the body alive.

When most people picture this survival response, they think of hyperarousal: a nervous system on high alert, with racing thoughts, tight muscles, anxiety, or explosive anger. But Guard Mode also has a quieter, more dangerous side. In hypoarousal, the system begins to shut down. The body goes heavy or numb, a person may feel far away or unreal, and basic functions like attention, digestion, and motivation go dim. This is where dissociation lives. Biologically, hypoarousal moves the nervous system closer to collapse and, over time, closer to death. It can be missed because it looks calm or "tired" on the outside, yet it often carries more risk than the visible, activated forms of Guard Mode we tend to notice first.

One of the most powerful counters to Guard Mode, on both the hyperarousal and hypoarousal ends of the spectrum, is relational play. Play that happens in the presence of an attuned, trustworthy other gives the nervous system a live experience of safety while it is still activated or shut down. For a hyperaroused system, relational play offers rhythm, humor, and shared focus that gently lowers intensity without demanding instant calm. For a hypoaroused system, relational play offers invitation, warmth, and small sparks of joy that help the body come back online. In both directions, it is the relationship inside the play that matters most. The nervous system learns, in real time, that it can move out of Guard Mode without being alone.

We often rush to respond to hyperarousal—the panic, anger, and agitation we can see. Hypoarousal is just as urgent. When a nervous system goes still, numb, or checked out, it is not giving up; it is fighting to stay alive by shutting down.

## Survival Before Identity

Children do not begin life asking, "Who am I?" They begin by asking, "Will someone come when I cry?"

Attachment science demonstrates that early caregiving shapes the developing brain's regulation systems, stress responses, and relational expectations across the lifespan. Long before identity forms, survival wiring is already in place.

Recent evidence shows that early life stress has lasting effects across physical health, cognitive development, emotional regulation, and social outcomes. These effects are shaped not only by isolated experiences but also by the environments in which children grow up. They are moderated by relational factors such as caregiver support and are accompanied by measurable biological changes. This evidence underscores the importance of early and collective preventive strategies.

Early life stress does not affect only one generation. It can shape how caregivers' bodies respond to stress, how they show up in relationships, and the conditions in which children are raised. These influences create intergenerational patterns of risk and resilience rather than isolated events. This is part of the reason trauma and chronic adversity often appear within family lines and communities. It is not because people are doomed, but because biology, behavior, and environment carry the imprint of what has been survived.

## The Lineage of the Brain Well-Being Model®

The Brain Well-Being Model® does not replace existing modalities. It expands them. In many ways, it grows from earlier traditions such as attachment theory, play therapy, Theraplay, ARC, polyvagal-informed science, and compassionate systems of awareness. It is grounded in neuroscience while remaining accessible to people without specialized licensure.

Attachment theory shows how early relationships create a secure base that shapes emotional regulation, trust, and the capacity to explore. Play therapy, Theraplay, and ARC translate that science into practical ways of using play, structure, and relationship to repair and strengthen bonds. Polyvagal-informed science explains how the autonomic nervous system constantly scans for danger or safety and shifts the body into states such as fight, flight, shutdown, or social engagement. Compassionate systems of awareness extend this knowledge into schools, organizations, and communities so that leaders can design environments that support regulation rather than undermine it.

The Brain Well-Being Model® weaves these threads into four simple and usable domains of awareness: somatic, perceptual, relational, and aspirational. These domains can be recognized by children, families, educators, community health workers, faith leaders, and clinicians in everyday life. While the earlier theories explain why safety and connection matter and how the nervous system responds, the Brain Well-Being Model® focuses on what to notice and practice in real time. It is a practical continuation of these traditions, designed to bring complex science into the places where people actually live, learn, work, and heal together.

The lineage of this model also reaches further back than contemporary neuroscience. In the early twentieth century, psychoanalyst Sándor Ferenczi challenged the rigid neutrality of classical analysis and argued for what we might now describe as radical empathy. He insisted that trauma was real, that early relational injury shaped development, and that healing required warmth, flexibility, and genuine partnership between healer and patient. Decades before attachment science and modern nervous system research provided biological explanations, Ferenczi recognized that safety is not created through distance but through attuned presence. The Brain Well-Being Model® stands within that relational tradition, honoring the insight that nervous systems heal in environments where empathy is embodied and where care is responsive rather than detached.

## A Classroom Story of Survival Learning

Imagine a child sitting in a crowded classroom. The room is loud. Chairs scrape across the floor. A frustrated teacher raises their voice. On paper, this child has been labeled "defiant" or "oppositional." They avoid eye contact, snap at peers, and refuse to begin assignments.

From the outside, it looks like a behavior problem. From the inside, the child's nervous system is in Guard Mode. Their body has learned, through past experiences, that raised voices and sudden movement can signal danger. Instead of opening to learn, the system tightens to survive.

When we understand this, the question shifts. Instead of asking, "What is wrong with this child?" we begin to ask, "What happened to this nervous system, and what does it need now to feel safe enough to learn?"

## When Stress Does Not End

Short-term stress is protective. Chronic stress is corrosive. Prolonged exposure to adversity, including poverty, racism, violence, illness, and community instability, creates biological wear known as allostatic load.

Over time, survival stops being temporary and becomes baseline. Protection becomes a pattern. The pattern can begin to shape identity.

## What Allostatic Load Feels Like in Everyday Life

Allostatic load is not only a scientific term used in research. It is how chronic stress shows up in daily living. It can appear as difficulty falling or staying asleep, frequent headaches or stomachaches, irritability that feels larger than the moment, or difficulty concentrating even on tasks a person cares about. Communities carrying heavy allostatic load may experience increased conflict, burnout, and hopelessness alongside remarkable creativity and resilience. None of these responses are signs of weakness. They are signs that bodies and systems have been working overtime to survive.

Today's youth are learning survival in a different landscape than previous generations. The nervous system is no longer responding only to what happens at home, school, or in the neighborhood. It is also reacting to a constant stream of images, alerts, and opinions arriving through phones and screens. Violent videos, crisis headlines, comparison culture, and constant notifications keep many young nervous systems in a state of low-grade Guard even when nothing dangerous is happening in the room. For youth growing up in the digital age, the question "Am I safe?" may be asked not once a day, but hundreds of times as new content appears, often without enough adult support or context to help their bodies settle again.

The Brain Well-Being Model® helps us see this not as individual weakness or "screen addiction," but as a nervous system trying to adapt to an environment that rarely gives it time to rest.

## The Three Modes of the Brain Well-Being Model®

In this book, the Brain Well-Being Model® describes three primary nervous system modes: Guard Mode, Healing Mode, and Thrive Mode. These modes are core components of the Brain Well-Being Index (BWI) and are assessed throughout the BWI as part of how brain well-being is understood and measured over time. These are not diagnoses. They are simple names for complex biological patterns that appear in everyday life and help us track where we are within the model at any given moment.

Guard Mode is the state the body enters when it senses danger, whether that danger is immediate or remembered. In Guard Mode, the nervous system prioritizes protection. Attention narrows. Muscles tense. The body moves toward fight, flight, freeze, or fawn. Guard Mode helped our ancestors survive and it still protects us today. However, when it becomes chronic, it can begin to take energy away from health, relationships, and imagination.

Healing Mode is the state the body moves toward when it experiences enough safety, rest, and support to begin unwinding from constant threat. In Healing Mode, the nervous system is still aware of danger, but it no longer runs the whole show. This is the core regulated band of the model. There is more space for curiosity, repair, and co-regulation. Sleep can deepen. Digestion can improve. Emotions become easier to tolerate. In the Brain Well-Being Index, Healing Mode reflects movement away from constant survival and toward increasing regulation and resilience over time.

Thrive Mode is the state in which safety has been stable long enough that the brain and body can invest energy in growth, creativity, and contribution. In Thrive Mode, the nervous system is still regulated, but now has surplus capacity for play, joy, learning, and long-term planning. We are more able to imagine the future, take healthy risks, and connect with others from a place of authenticity instead of survival. Within the BWI, Thrive Mode reflects sustained regulation with enough resource for expansion and flourishing, not just recovery.

Thrive Mode is not abstract. It shows up in small, specific moments when the body feels genuinely safe and free enough to enjoy being alive. For some people, Thrive Mode feels like warmth and sun on their face during a slow walk after a good meal, when their breath is easy, their shoulders have softened, and they can actually feel gratitude or joy instead of just thinking about it. In these moments, the nervous system is not only out of Guard Mode; it has enough surplus energy to notice beauty, savor connection, and feel renewed. Those brief experiences of Thrive, repeated over time, help refuel the work of Healing Mode.

One simple way to feel the difference between Healing and Thrive is to notice what your body is organized around. In Healing Mode, a walk might be about calming down after a hard day and finally feeling your shoulders drop. In Thrive Mode, that same walk might feel like being held by the day itself:

warmth on your face, a full belly, a sense of ease and possibility in your chest. In that moment, you are not only out of Guard Mode; you also know, in your body, what helped you get there—rest, food, movement, connection—which makes it easier to find your way back again.

Most people and communities move between these modes over time. We are not meant to live in any single state forever. The goal of this model is not to "banish" Guard Mode, but to help us recognize when it is running our lives and to build pathways back into Healing Mode and Thrive Mode, both individually and together, in ways that can be seen and supported through the Brain Well-Being Index. Progress does not mean never entering Guard Mode again. Progress means that Guard Mode episodes become less frequent, less intense, and shorter, and that it becomes easier to find our way back to regulation and connection each time. Brain well-being is measured less by whether Guard Mode appears and more by how quickly and safely we can move out of it and spend more of life in Healing and Thrive.

In this model of Brain Well-Being, Guard Mode, Healing Mode, and Thrive Mode are not fixed stages but recurring nervous-system states, and the work of healing is to move between them more efficiently over time, spending less of life in chronic Guard and more in sustainable safety and growth.

## Movement Between Guard, Healing, and Thrive Modes

Guard Mode, Healing Mode, and Thrive Mode are recurring nervous system states rather than fixed stages. This model maps the ongoing movement between them and orients us toward spending less time in chronic Guard and more time in sustainable safety, connection, and growth.

## The Question Beneath Every Symptom

Across therapy rooms, classrooms, hospitals, and homes, many different labels describe distress. Beneath those labels lives a quieter question:

What happened to this nervous system, and what does it need now to feel safe enough to grow?

Healing begins not with control but with safety. One of the oldest biological pathways back toward safety is something children understand instinctively: play.

## For Providers and Caregivers: Reflective Questions

As you consider the children, families, or communities you support, it may help to pause with questions such as these.

- Where do I see Guard Mode showing up, such as withdrawal, perfectionism, anger, people pleasing, or shutting down?
- Which behaviors have I previously labeled "noncompliant" or "difficult" that might actually be survival responses?
- How do the larger systems around this person, including schools, workplaces, neighborhoods, and policies, add to or reduce allostatic load?
- What small and consistent cues of safety can I offer more often, such as predictable routines, a warm tone of voice, repair after conflict, or clear choices?

Each nervous system you encounter is already doing its best to survive within the conditions it has been given. This chapter invites you to see those survival patterns not as the whole story but as the starting place for healing.

# Chapter 2

# Why Self Awareness Is the Foundation of Healing

Before skills, before tools, and before interventions, we begin with awareness.

Self-awareness is not only psychological insight. It is biological intelligence. It is the capacity to notice what the body, brain, and relationships are doing in real time instead of understanding them only in hindsight.

When people seek healing, they are often offered strategies before they are offered awareness. They are given scripts, coping skills, or behavior plans without first being taught how to feel their own internal signals. Yet it is difficult to shift a state that cannot be sensed. It is difficult to choose a new pattern if the current one cannot be recognized from the inside.

The Brain Well-Being Model follows this order because healing tends to unfold in a specific sequence. Awareness comes first, not because insight alone is enough, but because it opens the door for the changes that follow.

Self awareness allows us to recognize which mode we are in—Guard, Healing, or Thrive—and to make choices that support movement toward greater safety and possibility.

In this model, the goal is not to stay in one perfect state. The goal is to grow the awareness and support needed to move between modes with less harm and more care. Regulation means being able to recognize Guard Mode, access enough safety to return to Healing Mode, and, at times, expand into Thrive Mode. Over time, healthier nervous systems spend more minutes and hours in Healing and Thrive, and when Guard does appear, they do not stay there as long or as alone.

## The Order of Intentional Awareness

In the Brain Well-Being Model, awareness is the central practice because there are only a few domains we can directly influence. These include what we do with our bodies, how we relate to our thoughts, and the environments we choose or help create.

We cannot control every stressor, every system, or every outcome. We can, however, strengthen our capacity to notice and respond within these spheres.

The order of intentional awareness in this model is deliberate:

- Somatic awareness
- Perceptual awareness
- Relational awareness
- Aspirational awareness

We begin with somatic awareness because the body is where Guard Mode and safety register first. The nervous system reacts before the narrative forms. Sensations come before stories.

From there we move into perceptual awareness, which involves the interpretations, assumptions, and meanings the mind generates in response to those sensations.

Next comes relational awareness. As regulation increases, we become more able to notice how our nervous systems interact with others. We begin to see how co-regulation, misattunement, belonging, and threat appear between people.

Finally, we expand into aspirational awareness, reconnecting with vision, purpose, and possibility. This is where intention, contribution, and meaning can take root.

This sequence mirrors how healing often unfolds. We begin with what is closest—sensations and thoughts—and gradually widen the circle to include relationships and dreams for the future. Regulation makes reflection possible. Reflection makes connection possible. Connection makes purpose sustainable. The movement is cyclical rather than linear. Each layer strengthens the others.

Regulate the body. Somatic.
Clarify the story. Perceptual.
Strengthen connection. Relational.
Reclaim purpose. Aspirational.

## Why Self Awareness Works

Self awareness is effective because it interrupts the automatic loops that keep Guard Mode active. When the nervous system is activated and unobserved, it drives behavior from the background. We may snap, withdraw, overwork, or shut down without understanding why. Awareness introduces a small but powerful pause into that process. That pause creates the possibility of choice.

On a biological level, noticing sensations, naming emotions, and identifying thoughts can shift activity away from pure survival and toward regions of the brain involved in reflection and regulation.

On a relational level, awareness reduces misinterpretation. Instead of assuming, "They do not care about me," we might recognize, "My body is in Guard Mode right now," or "Their tone reminded me of an earlier hurt." This does not erase harm, but it expands the options for how we respond.

Over time, repeated moments of awareness become a practice. That practice changes patterns. When those changed patterns spread across families, classrooms, and communities, they begin to shape culture.

## 1. Somatic Awareness

You cannot change what you cannot feel. You cannot regulate what you cannot sense.

Somatic awareness is the first domain because, for most people, the body is where the truth appears first. Long before we can name our emotions or explain our history, the nervous system communicates through sensation and impulse. A tight jaw, a heavy chest, a racing mind, or a sudden urge to leave the room are all forms of communication from the body.

Many people take action only when the body finally becomes loud. The headache will not go away. The back pain flares. The fatigue becomes impossible to ignore. Panic seems to appear without warning. Somatic awareness invites us to listen earlier. It asks us to consider that the body has been communicating all along and that responding earlier may prevent the need for it to shout.

Somatic awareness means noticing signals instead of overriding them. Tight shoulders, a dropping stomach, racing thoughts, numbness, shutdown, buzzing energy, restlessness, or the foggy feeling that makes it difficult to think are not random inconveniences. They are the nervous system's way of signaling that something does not feel safe or that something needs care. These low-energy states are not laziness or lack of willpower; they are signs that the nervous system has moved beyond activation into shutdown, edging toward the same biological territory the body approaches when life is at risk. When we ignore hypoarousal, we overlook some of the most dangerous forms of Guard Mode precisely because they are quiet.

For many people, especially those who have survived trauma, racism, or chronic stress, these signals have been dismissed or punished. They may have been told to push through, stop being sensitive, or be strong even when their bodies were sending clear signals of overload. Over time, ignoring those signals can lead to burnout, illness, or a sense of disconnection from oneself. Somatic awareness offers a different pattern. It encourages curiosity instead of criticism and partnership with the body rather than conflict against it.

Simple practices can begin this reconnection. You might notice your feet on the ground, track where tension lives in your body, observe your breath without trying to change it, or stretch gently and then notice how your body responds. These practices are not about perfection. They are about building a relationship with your body in which you check in, listen, and respond.

As somatic awareness grows, something important shifts. Instead of realizing we are overwhelmed only after we have exploded, shut down, or dissociated, we begin to notice earlier cues. We might sense tightness in the chest before an argument, shallow breathing before a meeting, or numbness before agreeing to something we do not have the capacity for. This earlier awareness creates room for different choices, such as stepping outside, drinking water, asking for support, or saying "not right now" rather than abandoning our own needs.

Somatic awareness does not eliminate Guard Mode. It does, however, allow us to recognize when the body is moving into protection. With that recognition comes the possibility of responding with compassion and deciding what support is needed next.

## 2. Perceptual Awareness

Perceptual awareness is about storytelling. It involves the stories we tell ourselves about who we are, the stories we imagine others tell about us, the stories spoken when we are not present, and the stories that remain after we are gone.

These stories are powerful because they shape what we notice, how we interpret events, and what we believe is possible. A person who has spent much of life in Guard Mode may carry beliefs such as "I am too much," "I am not safe anywhere," or "People like me do not get happy endings." Another person who has grown up surrounded by support and representation may hold stories such as "My voice matters" or "My community has survived worse than this." Neither set of stories appears randomly. Each one is a survival map the brain has drawn from lived experience.

Perceptual awareness invites curiosity about these internal maps. It encourages us to ask questions such as:

- What story am I telling myself about this moment?

- Where did that story come from: my family, my culture, my history, media, or my own experiences?
- Does this story protect me, limit me, or both?

Stories do not exist only inside individuals. They also surround us through media, art, music, and public narratives about who is valued and who is not. Seeing ourselves reflected with dignity in books, films, and images can expand what we believe is possible. Being erased or stereotyped can quietly teach us that we do not belong.

Representation is not only about visibility. It is also about mental well-being. The images and stories that circulate around us influence the beliefs we carry about our worth, our future, and our place in the world.

Perceptual awareness, then, is not about judging our stories. It is about recognizing that they are stories, powerful and meaningful, and also capable of being revised. When we notice, "This is the old story speaking," we create enough space to imagine a different one. That shift in perception can change how a nervous system, a family, or an entire community moves through the world.

## 3. Relational Awareness

Relational awareness is where awareness begins to influence behavior in visible ways. It involves noticing not only how we feel inside but also how we show up with others and how our relationship with comfort itself can keep us stagnant.

Without relational awareness, we can remain loyal to patterns that feel familiar but keep us small. These patterns may include relationships that drain us, roles we have outgrown, expectations we never consciously chose, or habits that soothe us in the short term while taking something from us in the long term. We may come to see these patterns as "just how life is," when in reality they are the ways an unexamined nervous system has learned to survive.

Relational awareness asks different questions:

- How do I tend to react when I feel close to someone? When I feel threatened?
- What kinds of relationships feel comfortable to me, and are they actually nourishing or simply familiar?
- How do my Guard Mode patterns, such as shutting down, pleasing, attacking, or fixing, shape the people I attract and the relational dynamics I repeat?

This domain is often where meaningful behavior change becomes possible. Somatic and perceptual awareness help us feel and name what is happening. Relational awareness asks what we will do with that understanding in our connections and commitments. It might mean setting a boundary, initiating a difficult conversation, seeking support, or choosing a different kind of relationship than those we have known before.

Our relationship with comfort is important in this domain. Sometimes comfort reflects genuine regulation, rest, safety, and ease. At other times, comfort reflects avoidance, remaining where we are because change feels uncertain even when the current situation is slowly harming us. Relational awareness helps us discern the difference. It allows us to choose the discomfort that leads to growth instead of the comfort that keeps us in cycles of harm.

In this way, relational awareness may be one of the most influential domains for shifting from merely living to truly thriving. It is where inner work begins to reshape families, friendships, teams, and communities. When we can recognize our patterns in relationships and respond with intention rather than reflex, healing stops being only an internal idea and becomes a shared reality.

## 4. Aspirational Awareness

Aspirational awareness is where awareness begins to create direction. It is the place where we begin to think about action, not only reacting to what has happened but also envisioning what could happen next. In this domain, we begin to see the road ahead and the path toward our hopes, values, and visions.

When Guard Mode has been dominant, the future can feel very small. The focus becomes simply getting through the day or avoiding the next crisis. Aspirational awareness gently widens that horizon.

It invites questions such as:

- What kind of life, community, or world do I want to help build?
- What would thriving look and feel like in my body and my relationships?
- If nothing changed overnight, what is one small step in that direction?

Within this domain we begin to form goals and consider how we might move toward them. We become more aware of what we need, such as rest, mentorship, boundaries, resources, skills, and community support. We also begin to think more clearly about what must change in order for those needs to become possible.

Aspirational awareness does not require that we know every step. It simply asks us to name a direction and to recognize that our nervous system will need support as we move toward it.

This awareness allows us to see ourselves as active participants in our own story rather than characters shaped only by stress, history, or other people's choices. Hope becomes more than an emotion. It becomes the capacity to imagine something different and to organize our energy toward it.

When aspirational awareness is nourished alongside somatic, perceptual, and relational awareness, we gain more than coping strategies. We gain a sense of purpose and a felt belief that change, while difficult, is possible.

## Self-Awareness as Community Practice

Self awareness is sometimes framed as a private and individual project. In this model, it is understood as a community practice. When one person becomes more aware of their Guard Mode patterns, everyone around them gains a little more safety. There is one more adult who can pause instead of punish, one more teacher who can recognize dysregulation instead of disrespect, and one more leader who can choose repair instead of retaliation.

In collective settings such as churches, schools, youth programs, and neighborhood spaces, shared language around somatic, perceptual, relational, and aspirational awareness can transform self awareness into a group norm. People can say things like, "My body is buzzing right now," or "I am moving into shutdown," without shame. This kind of language normalizes nervous system literacy and makes it easier for people to ask for and offer support.

Community-centered healing does not mean that everyone feels calm all the time. It means that a group has enough shared awareness to notice when Guard Mode is taking over and enough shared commitment to help one another find the way back. In this way, self-awareness becomes a form of mutual care. Each person's practice strengthens the village.

## A First Glimpse of Collective Care in Action®

Self awareness is the foundation of healing, but it is not the finish line. Noticing your own nervous system is the first step. Learning to notice and care for one another's nervous systems is where Collective Care in Action® begins.

Collective Care in Action® is the community expression of the Brain Well-Being Model. It asks what happens when somatic, perceptual, relational, and aspirational awareness are practiced not only by individuals but also by families, classrooms, churches, clinics, and neighborhoods together. In this perspective, awareness is not a solitary project. It becomes shared language, shared ritual, and shared responsibility.

When one person learns to recognize their Guard Mode, they gain choices. When a group learns to recognize Guard Mode together, they gain culture. They can design spaces, routines, and practices that protect nervous systems rather than overwhelm them. They can build environments where rest, repair, play, and co-regulation are expected rather than earned.

This chapter has focused on awareness within the individual. In the chapters that follow, we will explore how that same awareness can move through communities, turning individual insight into collective healing.

## Why the Sequence Matters

This is why the sequence matters.

Safety first.
Meaning second.
Connection third.
Possibility last.

If we attempt to build skills, change behaviors, or set goals without first restoring awareness, we risk layering new tasks onto an already dysregulated system. Insight without somatic and relational support can even increase shame. People may understand why they are struggling while still feeling unable to change.

The Brain Well-Being Model mirrors both human development and human healing. Infants begin with bodies and signals, which corresponds to the somatic domain. They grow into perceptions and stories, which relate to the perceptual domain. They deepen into relationships, which reflects the relational domain. Eventually they reach toward purpose, contribution, and vision, which belongs to the aspirational domain.

Healing often retraces this arc in reverse. We return to the body, clarify our perceptions, repair relationships, and then rediscover what is possible.

## Reflection: Your Awareness Sequence

You might pause with a few reflective questions:

- Which domain feels easiest for you right now?
- Which domain feels blocked or difficult at the moment?
- How did your family model, or not model, these four domains?

What small practice could help you increase awareness today? For example: a body check-in, a story you choose to question, a conversation you decide to initiate, or a hope you allow yourself to name. You might also notice any small moments that already feel like Thrive—a meal that truly nourishes you, a walk in the sun, a laugh that reaches your body—and name them as such, so your nervous system learns to recognize that state on purpose.

Your awareness is not a small thing. It is the doorway through which every other form of healing can begin.

## A Space for Reflective Practice on Brain Well-Being

Use the space that follows to jot down any sensations, stories, relationships, or hopes that came up as you read. There is no right way to do this. Your awareness is enough.

# Chapter 3

# Play, Art, Gardening, and Music

## How Regulation Grows in Relationship

In Chapter 1, we explored why the brain learns survival first and how Guard Mode, Healing Mode, and Thrive Mode give us a simple language for the nervous system's main states. In Chapter 2, we named somatic, perceptual, relational, and aspirational awareness as the four domains that help us notice which mode we are in and what we might need next. This chapter begins to address the next question: how do we support the nervous system to move from Guard Mode toward Healing Mode and Thrive Mode in everyday life?

One of the most powerful answers is also one of the oldest: play.

## Regulation Grows in Relationship

Humans do not regulate alone. We regulate with one another. From infancy onward, the nervous system learns safety through relational cues such as:

• Eye contact

• Tone of voice

• Rhythm

• Predictability

• Caregiver presence

This process, known as co-regulation, forms the foundation of emotional health. Research in play therapy, attachment science, and polyvagal informed studies all converge on the same conclusion. Relationships are the mechanism of healing. Not technique. Not insight alone. Relationship.

When caregivers, teachers, peers, and community members offer steady and attuned presence, the nervous system receives repeated messages: you are not alone; your feelings make sense; we can handle this together. Over time, those messages become internalized. The nervous system gradually learns to hold more emotion, more experience, and more complexity without collapsing into Guard Mode.

## Why Play Heals the Brain

Play is not a break from healing. Play is one of the ways the brain and body carry out their healing work.

For both children and adults, play functions as a natural regulation system. Through play, the nervous system experiments with movement, rhythm, imagination, and relationship in a context that feels safe enough to explore.

When people play through games, music, art, gardening, sports, or imaginative storytelling, the body begins to shift out of constant vigilance and into states where curiosity and connection become possible. Muscles soften. Breathing deepens. Laughter and creative focus gently move energy away from Guard Mode and toward Healing Mode. Over time, repeated experiences of safe play strengthen the pathways associated with Thrive Mode, including joy, learning, flexibility, and hope.

This is one reason play therapy is so effective. Children often process difficult experiences through dolls, blocks, drawing, and imaginative play rather than through lectures or explanations. Adults also seek similar pathways when life feels overwhelming. Concerts, game nights, dance classes, creative workshops, and joyful community gatherings often serve as informal spaces of regulation and renewal.

The nervous system remembers that play can be a doorway back to balance.

## Why the Body Must Go First

Before the mind constructs meaning, the body registers safety or danger.

Body first.

Story second.

Always.

Chronic stress, trauma, and modern overstimulation affect the nervous system long before a person can explain what they are feeling. A child may say "I'm fine" while their jaw is clenched and their stomach hurts. An adult may insist that something is not a big deal while their heart races and their sleep disappears.

When survival biology takes over, the thinking brain becomes less available and the body becomes the first witness to both pain and possibility.

This is why the Brain Well Being Model® begins with somatic awareness. Guard Mode cannot be shifted by logic alone. The nervous system needs experiences of safety, not only explanations of safety.

## The Nervous System as Translator

The nervous system acts as a translator between the outer world and our inner life. The vagus nerve, sensory pathways, breathing patterns, and muscle tone all influence perception before conscious thoughts appear.

When the body is dysregulated, the mind interprets the world through a narrow lens. A neutral face may appear threatening. Silence may feel like rejection. A small mistake may feel catastrophic.

When the body softens, the mind begins to reopen.

Many forms of play communicate directly with the nervous system:

- **Art and expressive arts:** Drawing, painting, collage, drumming, singing, and movement offer nonverbal ways to release and process emotion and energy. These activities invite creativity without requiring right answers, which helps Guard Mode relax.

- **Gardening and nature play:** Digging, planting, watering, harvesting, and simply spending time with plants support regulation through rhythm, sensory input, sunlight, and connection with living systems. These activities become forms of play with the earth.

- **Music and rhythm:** Clapping games, drumming, chanting, group singing, and listening to music together create shared patterns that support co regulation and social engagement. Humming can gently stimulate the vagus nerve, helping the body shift out of guard mode and into a calmer, regulated state where the nervous system can rest, reset, and feel safe.

- **Sensory and movement play:** Soil, water, paint, clay, swings, dancing, and bilateral movement such as walking or rocking help the body complete stress cycles and discover new patterns of ease.

Even structured trauma-focused methods draw on these same principles. Approaches like EMDR and brainspotting use bilateral stimulation and focused body awareness to help the brain process stored traumatic material while keeping one foot in the present. They pair movement, rhythm, and focused attention with safety so that the nervous system can move toward resolution.

None of these practices require someone to explain what they feel in perfect sentences. They allow the body to speak first, and they meet the nervous system where it lives: in sensation, rhythm, and relationship.

## Art and Gardening as Nervous System Medicine

Two practices sit at the heart of this model's approach to regulation: art and gardening. They are not just creative hobbies; they are nervous system experiences that reach all four domains of awareness at once.

Research on gardening shows that tending plants and spending time in gardens can reduce stress and anxiety, improve mood, increase a sense of purpose, and build social connection and resilience. People who garden regularly often report higher life satisfaction and lower perceived stress than those who do not. Community gardening in particular has been linked to stronger social ties and greater emotional resilience in neighborhoods.

Art and expressive arts show similar patterns. Creative expression engages sensory and emotional parts of the brain that do not rely only on words, allowing the nervous system to process experiences that may be hard to talk about. Rhythmic and bilateral movements in art-making—like drawing with both hands, drumming, or repeating brushstrokes—support regulation and integration after trauma. Working with color, image, sound, and movement creates symbolic distance, so people can approach painful material without overwhelming the system.

Within the Brain Well-Being Model®, gardening and art are not "extras" for people who already feel well.

<u>They are doorways into Healing Mode and Thrive Mode that honor all four awareness domains:</u>

- *Somatic:* hands in soil, breath in fresh air, muscles moving, senses engaged.

- *Perceptual:* new stories about oneself as a creator, a grower, a contributor to beauty or nourishment.

- *Relational:* shared plots, shared murals, shared songs, shared rituals that build co-regulation and belonging.

- *Aspirational:* imagining a future harvest, a finished piece, or a transformed space, and seeing tangible proof that care today can change tomorrow.

For communities who have been historically denied land, representation, or safe spaces to create, gardening and art also become acts of reclamation. They say: our bodies, our stories, and our environments matter. Our nervous systems deserve places to rest, to play, and to imagine more than survival.

## Adults Deserve Play Too

Many adults turn toward:

- brunch with friends

- hikes

- yoga

- art classes

- gardening

- travel

- community rituals

not as hobbies, but as forms of nervous system recovery. Their bodies are seeking spaces where Guard Mode can loosen: laughter at a table, sunlight on skin, music in a room, shared ritual in a sanctuary or community space.

Play is not childish.

Play is how adults come home to themselves.

When adults have access to play, rest, and co-regulation, they are more able to offer those same experiences to children and communities. Regulation flows both directions: children borrow nervous system stability from adults, and adults can rediscover regulation through moments of genuine play with children, peers, and elders.

## The Brain Well-Being Model® in Daily Life

The Brain Well-Being Model® is meant to give families, classrooms, clinics, and communities a shared language for these processes.

<u>The Brain Well-Being Model® helps people ask:</u>

- What is happening in the body (somatic)?

- What story is being told about this moment (perceptual)?

- What is happening between us, nervous system to nervous system (relational)?

- What are we moving toward together (aspirational)?

When people use this language, regulation stops being a mysterious skill some people "have" and others "lack." It becomes something that can be practiced, taught, and shared. A classroom can build daily rituals that support downshifting from Guard Mode. A family can design a "regulation corner" with art supplies, sensory tools, and plants. A community program can weave in rhythm, movement, and gardening as core curriculum, not side activities.

### *Play Now. Thrive Later.* in Practice

The philosophy at the heart of this book, *Play Now. Thrive Later.*, is not a slogan; it is a neurobiological truth. When we invest in play, art, gardening, and music now, we are literally building the brain pathways that make Thrive Mode possible later. We are teaching nervous systems—especially those shaped by trauma and chronic stress—that joy, rest, curiosity, and connection are not luxuries. They are part of health.

Now that we have grounded ourselves in the body and seen how regulation grows through relationship, play, art, gardening, and music, we can widen the lens of perception. Chapter 1 named the cost of living in Guard Mode. Chapter 2 named awareness as the foundation of change. This chapter has shown how everyday practices, especially play-based ones, give the nervous system real experiences of Healing Mode and glimpses of Thrive Mode.

In the chapters that follow, we will deepen each domain of the Brain Well-Being Model® and explore how Collective Care in Action® brings these practices into schools, families, clinics, faith communities, and youth programs, so play and regulation become not just individual coping strategies, but community norms.

## Reflection & Practice

*For Self*

Try one somatic, creative, or nature-based practice from this chapter and notice your body's response. What changed, even slightly, in your breath, muscles, or thoughts?

*For Families*

Do a three-minute "regulation reset" after school or work: a shared stretch, song and dance, watering plants together, or quiet drawing at the table.

*For Classrooms/Youth Programs*

Add rhythm or micro-movement between transitions: a clapping pattern, a breathing count, a brief stretch, or a one-minute "shake it out" before instruction resumes.

*For Systems/Organizations*

Start meetings with grounding or breath. Even thirty seconds of collective pause can shift the tone of decision-making and remind everyone present that nervous systems are in the room, not just job titles.

# Chapter 4

# Guard Mode and the Weight of History

The Brain Well-Being Model® began with a simple observation: Guard Mode is not only a personal state. It is also a social and historical one. Bodies do not learn to remain on alert in isolation. They learn within families, communities, and systems that are either predictable and protective or chaotic and threatening.

Up to this point, we have explored Guard Mode mainly at the individual level through early stress, nervous system states, and the four awareness domains. To understand why many people never fully leave Guard Mode, we now need to zoom out. We must ask what kinds of neighborhoods, schools, workplaces, and health systems make it difficult for the body to ever feel fully safe.

Public health and equity research describe this broader landscape in clear terms. Structural racism, community disinvestment, environmental harm, and medical inequity are not abstract concepts. They are conditions that raise allostatic load, shorten life expectancy, and keep entire populations living closer to survival than to thriving. When policy and history make safety unpredictable, Guard Mode becomes a community pattern rather than an individual exception.

I focus on Los Angeles County, and specifically on Black Los Angeles, for three reasons. First, this is home. It is where I live, raise my son, and run two community based organizations. The patterns described here are rooted in relationships, not distant observation.

Second, the County has made a rare and important decision to study Black life directly through its Anti-Racism, Diversity, and Inclusion (ARDI) Initiative and the *State of Black Los Angeles County* reports. These efforts emerged after the Board of Supervisors adopted an anti-racist policy agenda in 2020. The reports bring together more than one hundred indicators drawn from census data, surveys, interviews, focus groups, and geospatial analysis. They examine how Black residents are actually faring across the life course in housing, health, education, economic opportunity, and civic life.

Third, the findings provide a living illustration of Guard Mode. They show Black Angelenos experiencing some of the most severe outcomes in the County across health and economic indicators while also revealing signs of well-being, resilience, and civic engagement that traditional metrics often overlook.

Los Angeles County offers a vivid example, and it also offers unusually detailed data. The *State of Black Los Angeles County* trends analysis describes life for Black residents as a combination of meaningful progress in some areas and deepening crises in others. Black residents are the only racial group to report a decrease in depression rates in recent years, and high school graduation rates have increased. At the same time, life expectancy has declined, poverty has increased, and homelessness has risen sharply. Black Los Angeles is a place where the biology of Guard Mode, the weight of history, and the power of collective care are all visible at once.

The ideas in this chapter did not begin as theory. They began as questions I was asking in therapy rooms, classrooms, church basements, wellness labs, and living rooms where Black children, parents, elders, and healers were already practicing survival, adaptation, and healing every day. What emerged was not simply a framework, but a clearer way of naming patterns I had been witnessing across generations, relationships, and systems.

In the pages that follow, we will look more closely at how Guard Mode is shaped by history and systems, how perception shifts under prolonged threat, and why culturally intelligent collective care is necessary if we want the Brain Well-Being Model® and Collective Care in Action® to matter beyond the clinic. Later, we will return to Black Los Angeles as a collective illustration of Guard Mode, using local data and lived stories to show how the Brain Well-Being Model® and Collective Care in Action® operate at the community level. Here we are laying the foundation, connecting the biology of Guard Mode to the weight of history so the model can meet people where they actually live.

## Perceptual Awareness Under Pressure

Earlier chapters introduced somatic awareness, the body as the first witness to safety or threat. Perceptual awareness asks a different question: once the body senses something, what story does the brain tell about it?

Perception is not neutral. It is shaped by history, context, emotion, culture, and nervous system state. Under conditions of safety, perception is flexible. People can hold multiple perspectives, tolerate uncertainty, and remain curious. Under threat, perception narrows. The brain prioritizes speed over nuance, certainty over complexity, and protection over openness.

This narrowing is not a moral failure. It is biology. Research on early and chronic adversity shows that repeated stress recalibrates stress response systems and changes how the brain evaluates and responds to the environment. Work on allostatic load demonstrates that repeated activation of stress responses over time alters hormones, inflammation, attention, and expectation. The more a nervous system has been required to survive, the more likely it is to view the world through a Guard Mode lens. For many communities, that lens has been shaped not only by personal experience but also by events that occurred long before anyone currently alive was born.

## When Trauma Writes on the Body

For many families and communities, Guard Mode did not begin with the current generation. It began with war, slavery, displacement, genocide, famine, and state sanctioned violence that left entire lineages prepared for danger. History appears in story and behavior, but it can also appear in biology.

Over the past two decades, trauma researchers and epigenetic scientists have begun to document how severe and prolonged stress can leave chemical marks on DNA that influence how stress response genes behave. These marks do not change the letters of the genetic code. Instead, they affect how easily certain genes, particularly those involved in the body's cortisol and HPA axis stress systems, are activated or suppressed.

In several human studies involving genocide survivors, war affected families, and individuals exposed to severe early adversity, scientists have found altered methylation patterns on key stress regulation genes such as **FKBP5** and **NR3C1**, which help regulate how the body responds to cortisol and recovers from stress. These epigenetic shifts have been observed not only in survivors but also in their children and, in some studies, in grandchildren who never experienced the original trauma themselves.

This does not mean that people are genetically destined to repeat what their ancestors endured. Instead, it suggests that emotional pain can become biologically embedded, shaping baseline Guard Mode in the nervous system even before a child is born. It helps explain why some children appear to enter the world with heightened stress sensitivity even in families that are providing care, protection, and love.

The hopeful dimension of this science is that epigenetic marks are not fixed destiny. Emerging research suggests that supportive relationships, enriched environments, and effective therapeutic interventions can influence methylation patterns at some of these stress related sites over time. In other words, just as trauma can leave molecular traces, healing experiences can begin to reshape how stress response genes function.

In the language of this book, epigenetics offers one biological pathway through which Guard Mode can be transmitted across generations. It also helps explain why Healing Mode and Thrive Mode must be cultivated not only for individuals but for families and communities across time. Healing does not erase what ancestors endured, but it can transform how those histories are carried in the bodies of people living today and in the generations that follow.

## How Guard Mode Shapes Meaning

When Guard Mode is active, the brain's primary task becomes survival. Attention narrows toward potential danger. Ambiguity feels unsafe. Difference may feel threatening. The nervous system searches for patterns that confirm risk and often ignores information that complicates the story.

In this state, assumptions can harden into beliefs.

Beliefs can harden into identities.

Identities can harden into oppositional narratives.

Guard Mode does not simply make people reactive. It can make stories rigid.

People in Guard Mode are not incapable of insight. Rather, their perception has been shaped under sustained pressure. Writer and social critic James Baldwin argued that a country cannot subject Black people to brutality and confinement without becoming something monstrous itself. His insight pointed to how a society organized around racial threat distorts perception on all sides. Journalist and author Ta-Nehisi Coates has similarly described learning to inhabit his body as a target, not because of personal paranoia but because of the real risks Black children face in American streets and schools.

When Guard Mode dominates, new information is filtered through existing threat narratives and may be dismissed or weaponized. Reasoning alone rarely changes minds when fear is high. Perceptual awareness does not require people to abandon their beliefs. Instead, it invites them to examine how those beliefs formed and what nervous system state those beliefs are protecting.

## Cognitive Distortion as a Stress Response

Many patterns labeled "cognitive distortions" in therapy, such as catastrophizing, black-and-white thinking, and overgeneralization, are often stress responses rather than simple thinking errors. Under prolonged threat, the brain simplifies. It creates binaries because binaries are easier to defend. It favors certainty because uncertainty feels dangerous. It scans for worst-case scenarios because preparation once mattered.

These patterns are not signs of irrationality.

They are signs of a system doing its best to protect itself.

When Black families in South LA expect systems to fail them, or prepare for danger even in ordinary interactions, they are often drawing from a long archive of experience: denied care, disrespectful treatment, lost loved ones, and institutional betrayal. The nervous system remembers what lived data has taught it.

Perceptual awareness allows us to notice when these patterns are active without shaming them. It creates a small space between stimulus and story. In that space, flexibility can return, but only if safety is present.

## Environments, Information Overload, and Collective Guard Mode

Modern environments place unprecedented demands on perception. Constant information flow, social media amplification, algorithmic outrage, and rapid cycles of crisis overwhelm the brain's ability to contextualize. Youth in particular are exposed to continuous imagery of violence, disaster, and comparison long before they have the developmental tools to process it.

In this landscape, Guard Mode is reinforced daily. Attention is fragmented. Emotional content is prioritized. Nuance is lost. Fear spreads faster than understanding. The nervous system is rarely given time to settle before the next stimulus arrives.

For Black Angelenos, these pressures land on top of existing structural stressors. County surveys show Black residents facing disproportionate inequities in access to health care, insurance coverage, and stable housing, which results in higher rates of physical and mental health problems. When the baseline environment is already saturated with threat, information overload can make Guard Mode feel permanent.

Perceptual awareness, therefore, requires more than individual intention. It requires environments that support pacing, context, and integration. Within the Brain Well-Being Model®, somatic awareness and regulation are the foundation. Only when bodies feel safe enough can perception widen, stories soften, and new meanings become possible.

## Racism, Bias, and Threat-Based Narratives

Some of the most enduring and damaging perceptual distortions are not individual at all. They are structural.

Racism, classism, and other forms of systemic oppression are sustained by narratives rooted in threat perception: stories about who belongs, who is dangerous, who deserves protection, and who does not. These narratives are reinforced culturally and institutionally, often long after their original conditions have changed.

Joy DeGruy's work on Post Traumatic Slave Syndrome describes how centuries of racial terror created protective behaviors such as hypervigilance, perfectionism, and mistrust that are still often misread as pathology rather than survival. Resmaa Menakem shows how racialized trauma lives in the body, and how what he calls white-body supremacy shapes not only what Black, brown, and Indigenous people must endure, but also how white bodies respond to discomfort and difference.

When local governments declare racism a public-health crisis, they are recognizing that these threat-based narratives have biological consequences across the life course. Guard Mode is not just a psychological metaphor. It is a public-health reality.

Perceptual awareness in this context is not about positive thinking. It is about learning to see the water we are swimming in: to recognize how stories about danger and worth have been constructed, whose interests they serve, and how they live in our bodies.

## Culturally Intelligent Care and Collective Care in Action®

In this landscape, culturally intelligent care moves beyond cultural competence or inclusion. It asks four core questions.

What has this community survived?

What strengths already exist here?

What healing traditions are present?

How do systems become trustworthy again?

Healing cannot occur without historical truth. bell hooks describes love as an act of will, both an intention and an action, and insists that love worthy of the name must confront injustice rather than look away. Maya Angelou's work testifies to the power of voice, story, and community in reclaiming dignity after violence. Together, they remind us that love, dignity, and voice are not luxuries. They are survival tools in the face of dehumanizing systems.

Culturally intelligent care honors this lineage. It recognizes that communities already hold practices of regulation and repair through church, music, mutual aid, gardening, storytelling, play, and everyday acts of protection, even when those practices have been dismissed by mainstream systems.

Across the United States, however, health care systems are often fragmented, confusing, and prohibitively expensive, especially for communities who would benefit most from culturally rooted care. The very approaches that build trust and improve outcomes, including community health workers, promotoras, and cultural brokers, have historically been underfunded, inconsistently reimbursed, or treated as add-ons rather than essential services. This creates gaps that families try to fill with one another. Neighbors, faith communities, barbershops, aunties, and community-based organizations quietly do the work of regulation and navigation without formal recognition.

The Brain Well-Being Model® and Collective Care in Action® were developed in response to those gaps. They offer a shared language that helps us notice when someone needs help, make it safer for people to accept help, and organize care around trust, relationship, and cultural intelligence rather than around crisis alone.

## Restoring Perceptual Flexibility and Collective Imagination

Perceptual awareness is restored not by forcing optimism or denying reality, but by creating conditions where the nervous system can tolerate complexity again. This happens when bodies are more regulated, relationships feel safer, time is slowed, and multiple truths are allowed to coexist. Play, art, gardening, dialogue, and shared reflection are powerful here. They do not work because they persuade. They work because they soften rigidity and allow meaning to emerge rather than be imposed.

In Community Play Dates, ARTGard studios, and wellness labs, children, youth, and adults experience the four awareness domains—somatic, perceptual, relational, and aspirational—in embodied ways. These spaces give Black families and other communities a chance to practice new stories about safety, belonging, and possibility without erasing what has been survived.

When perception becomes more flexible, curiosity returns. When curiosity returns, connection becomes possible. Danger does not disappear, but it is no longer the only lens through which the world is seen.

## Bridge Forward: Preparing for the Collective Illustration

Perceptual awareness bridges the body and relationships. It translates sensation into story and story into action. When perception is rigid, relationships fracture. When perception softens, connection becomes possible again.

Understanding Guard Mode biologically and historically is only the beginning. The next question is practical.

How do individuals and communities move toward healing and thriving in real environments, especially when those environments have been shaped by centuries of threat?

The chapters that follow turn toward relational and aspirational awareness: how safety is experienced between people, how connection regulates the nervous system, and how hope and purpose re-emerge after prolonged stress. This book later presents a deeper collective illustration, drawing from national and Los Angeles-based research and lived narratives to examine Guard Mode at the community nervous-system level. It is not a single clinical case report, but an integration of data and story that makes the model visible in everyday Black life.

Perception shapes relationships.

Relationships reshape perception.

Chapter 5

# The Brain Well-Being Model®: From Survival to Thriving

By the time we reach this point in the journey, one reality becomes clear. Human distress is not random. It is patterned: biological, relational, historical, and environmental. Because distress follows patterns, healing must also follow patterns. These are not rigid formulas but reliable pathways the nervous system can learn to trust.

The Brain Well-Being Model® emerged from this need. It translates decades of neuroscience, trauma research, attachment science, somatic practice, play therapy, and community healing traditions into something people can use in everyday life, especially in communities carrying heavy Guard Mode. It is not a theory to admire. It is a map to follow.

**Why the Model Is Necessary**

Modern mental health systems often separate what was never meant to be separated. The body is treated apart from the mind. The individual is treated apart from the community. Symptoms are treated apart from history. Clinical care is treated apart from culture. Healing is treated as an endpoint instead of an ongoing process.

The nervous system does not function in fragments. It functions through integration. A well-designed model does not reduce complexity. Instead, it organizes complexity so that healing becomes repeatable, teachable, and shareable across different environments. These environments include therapy rooms, classrooms, homes, churches, community spaces, health systems, streets, gardens, and playgrounds.

Awareness serves as the bridge between sensation and interpretation. When awareness expands, rigid thinking begins to loosen. The nervous system becomes more capable of flexible responses rather than automatic reactions. The four awareness domains work together to help individuals and communities move from Guard Mode back toward connection, creativity, and choice.

The Central Movement: Survival → Regulation → Connection → Purpose

Somatic → Perceptual → Relational → Aspirational

(See Figure 1: The Brain Well-Being Model® Flow)

Movement Between Guard, Healing, and Thrive Modes

## Moving Through the Mode States

*Guard → Healing → Thrive*

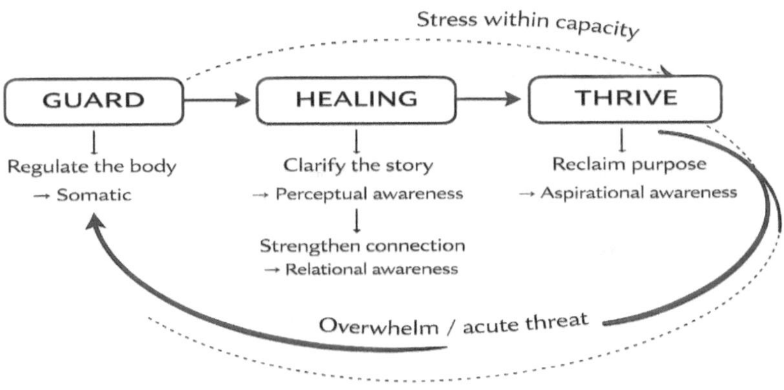


Mobility, not perfection.

At its core, the model describes a directional flow inside human development and healing. Not a straight line. Not a permanent state. But a recurring movement:

- Survival protects life.

- Regulation stabilizes the body.

- Connection restores relationship.

- Purpose reopens the future.

Although this movement is presented in a sequence, it is not linear in real life. People and communities circle through survival, regulation, connection, and purpose many times. Sometimes the body settles first. Sometimes a relationship or a sense of purpose arrives before physical calm. The model is a compass, not a staircase. In earlier chapters, this sequence showed up as Guard Mode, Healing Mode, and Thrive Mode; here, the Brain Well-Being Model® gathers those pieces into one consistent map we will return to throughout the book.

Awareness restores regulation.

Regulation restores choice.

Choice restores humanity.

## The Four Domains of Awareness

### 1. Somatic Awareness

The body is the first site of safety. Before thoughts change, before beliefs shift, before relationships repair, the nervous system must experience felt regulation, slightly deeper breaths, loosening muscles, a sense that it is safe enough to stay present. Somatic awareness is the ability to notice and interpret these signals instead of overriding them.

## 2. Perceptual Awareness

How the brain interprets reality. Once the body stabilizes, perception can soften. Threat is no longer the only lens. Possibility, nuance, and new stories about self and community become visible again. Perceptual awareness is our capacity to notice the stories we are telling and to recognize that they were shaped, not destined.

## 3. Relational Awareness

Safety experienced with other people. Humans regulate in connection, not isolation. No nervous system heals alone for long; co-regulation, repair after conflict, trustworthy presence, and culturally rooted belonging become part of how Guard Mode unwinds. Relational awareness helps us see how our patterns show up with others, and how we can practice new ones.

## 4. Aspirational Awareness

The return of future orientation and purpose. When survival quiets and connection becomes trustworthy, the future reopens. Thriving is not the absence of pain. It is the presence of possibility, direction, and a felt sense that one's life and community can still grow. Aspirational awareness is where values, dreams, and collective visions begin to shape daily choices. Hope returns. Possibility reshapes the ability to take action toward goals.

These domains are related in both sequence and circle. Often, somatic awareness opens perceptual awareness, which deepens relational awareness, which reignites aspirational awareness. At other times, a renewed sense of purpose pulls someone back toward relationships and body-based practices. However the sequence unfolds, the four domains keep influencing one another.

## Environments Shape Awareness

Awareness does not grow in a vacuum. It is shaped by environments that either keep nervous systems in Guard Mode or invite them toward Healing Mode and Thrive Mode.

<u>Awareness grows in:</u>

- predictable routines

- enriched environments and sensory-safe spaces

- safe relationships and trusted adults

- spaces where emotions can move without punishment

- play, art, nature, rhythm, and gardening

- cultural/ancestral practices, community rituals and collective care traditions

These conditions are not extras. They are the soil in which somatic, perceptual, relational, and aspirational awareness can take root and expand.

## Cycling Through Modes Is Normal

Humans are not meant to stay in Thrive Mode all the time. We cycle. Health is not permanently calm. Health is the ability to return, to move through Guard, Healing, and Thrive Mode in many directions over time without getting permanently stuck in any one state.

Most people and communities move through these modes many times across a day, a year, and a lifetime. In that sense, Guard Mode is not the enemy of healing; it is part of the story that reminds us why reliable pathways and supportive environments matter.

## Measurement, Reflection, and the Brain Well-Being Index

If healing is real, it must be observable. The Brain Well-Being Index (BWI) was developed as a reflective tool aligned with the four awareness domains, not to label people, but to help individuals and communities notice growth in Guard, Healing, and Thrive Mode over time.

The BWI focuses on state shifts rather than only symptoms: small changes in somatic ease, perceptual flexibility, relational safety, and aspirational orientation are understood as meaningful biological and relational change, especially in high-Guard environments. Later chapters explore how the BWI functions in clinical care, schools, wellness labs, ARTGard environments, and home-based wellness kits, and Appendix A provides a technical overview of the tool.

## The Bridge to Practice

A model alone does nothing. It becomes real only when it enters daily environments: a classroom drum circle, a therapy session, a community garden, a church resource fair, a barbershop or salon, or a wellness kit opened at a kitchen table. This is where theory becomes Collective Care in Action® and where the Brain Well-Being Model® begins to live in the hands of families, youth, and practitioners.

The chapters that follow explore how this happens in practice. We will look at where healing is already taking place, how environments can be designed so the brain can experience well being, and how the movement from Guard Mode to Healing Mode unfolds in real time for individuals, families, and communities.

# Chapter 6

# Where Healing Is Already Happening

Long before a model is named, healing is already taking place somewhere. It happens in classrooms where a teacher pauses long enough for a child's nervous system to settle. It happens in living rooms where a grandmother hums softly without calling it regulation. It happens in church basements, barbershops, beauty salons, community gardens, and crowded apartment kitchens where people hold one another through stress that has no clinical language.

Healing rarely begins in institutions. It begins in a relationship. It begins wherever bodies feel just safe enough to breathe a little deeper, wherever stories can be told without punishment, and wherever people are allowed to be human rather than only productive. Across attachment research, relational neurobiology, and community healing traditions, the message is consistent: regulation grows in connection long before it is formalized into programs.

## Regulation Before Interpretation

The nervous system must feel safer before insight can lead to meaningful change. Without safety, reflection feels threatening, learning feels overwhelming, connection feels risky, and joy can feel unfamiliar. This helps explain why many well intentioned interventions struggle in communities carrying chronic stress. They often begin with education before regulation, compliance before relationship, and services before trust.

Where safety increases, capacity increases. Where safety is absent, even the best resources remain unused. What appears to be resistance or non engagement is often Guard Mode doing exactly what it was designed to do: protecting a nervous system that has learned, over time, that new programs and promises do not always mean real safety. Trauma and toxic stress research describe this as adaptation to the environment rather than personal failure.

In the Brain Well Being Model®, this means that somatic and relational awareness must be supported first. Bodies and relationships need enough predictability, warmth, and repair for perceptual and aspirational awareness to begin opening. Only then can new information, skills, or opportunities be fully received.

## Community Spaces as Nervous System Environments

Places regulate bodies whether intentionally or not. Every environment teaches the nervous system something about safety, worth, and belonging. A loud and unpredictable waiting room with harsh lighting and rushed staff may keep Guard Mode active, regardless of how excellent the services appear on paper. A modest room with familiar faces, music that feels like home, and a predictable rhythm may do far more to support regulation than a perfectly designed manual.

The deeper question becomes: What environments does a person live inside every single day, and what do those places teach their body about itself? For many people, especially in communities of color, the most powerful regulation spaces have never been labeled as such. They include:

- A youth room where adults remember names and show up consistently.

- A choir rehearsal where breath and rhythm synchronize across generations.

- A community garden where hands in soil reconnect people to land and lineage.

- A Sunday meal where elders tell stories that make survival feel honorable instead of shameful.

- A barbershop or salon where someone asks, "How are you really?" and stays to hear the answer.

Play therapy, expressive arts, community gardening, and Black literary and spiritual traditions have long recognized these spaces as sites of real healing, even when systems overlook them. These are not side notes to healing. They are some of its primary locations.

## Enriched Environments in Everyday Life

Neuroscience and developmental science sometimes use the term enriched environment to describe settings that offer consistent safety, sensory nourishment, and opportunities for exploration and relationship. In the Brain Well-Being Model®, enriched environments are not elite programs; they are everyday spaces where somatic, perceptual, relational, and aspirational awareness can grow at the same time.

An enriched environment might look like:

- A classroom with predictable openings and closings, soft corners, and sensory tools that are allowed, not punished.

- A choir, drum circle, or dance group where rhythm, movement, and voice regulate the body without requiring people to talk about their pain first.

- A community garden where planting, watering, and harvesting create a shared rhythm, and where growth is visible even when life feels stuck.

- A salon or barbershop where touch, story, music, and cultural care allow nervous systems to downshift, even when the outside world has not changed.

These environments engage all four awareness domains. Bodies move and settle (somatic). Meanings and stories shift through art, music, conversation, and reflection (perceptual). Relationships form and deepen, making co-regulation and belonging possible (relational). Futures are imagined together, whether in the form of a new hairstyle, a child's dream, or a community vision (aspirational).

Art studios and gardens are themselves living systems. They respond to how they are tended and who is present. When people create together on a canvas or share labor in a garden bed, they become part of a small ecosystem of energy, attention, and care. In those moments, no one has to "get it right" for the nervous system to benefit. The act of showing up, moving hands, and being witnessed is often enough to begin shifting Guard Mode toward Healing Mode.

## How Art Supports Regulation and Connection

In this model, art is not decoration; it is a regulatory practice. Making art—drawing, painting, sculpting, collaging, moving—engages the senses, recruits both sides of the brain, and offers a way to express what cannot yet be put into words. For many people, especially those living with chronic stress or trauma, it is safer to start with color, shape, and movement than with direct storytelling.

Art-making can:

- Give the body repetitive, soothing actions (brush strokes, cutting, gluing) that support somatic awareness and calming.

- Offer symbols and metaphors that help people see their situation from a different angle, supporting perceptual awareness.

- Build connections when done in groups, as people create side-by-side, share materials, and witness each other's work, strengthening relational awareness.

- Open aspirational awareness as people imagine, design, and complete something that did not exist before, practicing agency and creativity.

Group art spaces also support co-regulation. Shared creative tasks activate social engagement: people glance at each other, mirror posture or pace, laugh at similar moments, and share small risks together. The nervous system recognizes this as a kind of safety that is physically felt, not just intellectually understood.

## How Gardening Supports Regulation and Connection

Gardening and nature-based practices function as living ecosystems of regulation. Working with soil, seeds, water, and sunlight offers rhythmic, repetitive, sensory input that settles the nervous system while reconnecting people to cycles larger than their immediate stress.

Gardening can:

- Ground somatic awareness through touch (soil, leaves, water), smell, and gentle physical effort, giving the body clear, present-moment signals.

- Shift perception by making growth and change visible over time; what looks barren in one season may be flourishing in the next.

- Deepen relational awareness through shared tasks—watering, harvesting, sharing food—and through intergenerational work in the garden.

- Nourish aspirational awareness as people envision what the space could become, plan plantings, and imagine who will benefit from the harvest.

For communities whose relationship with land has been disrupted by colonization, enslavement, displacement, or environmental racism, nature-based regulation also carries cultural and historical meaning. Gardening, walking, and simply being with trees or the ocean can become acts of reclamation:

reminders that the nervous system is connected to land, sky, and water that existed long before the systems that cause harm.

## The Return of Collective Healing

Across systems, the direction of real healing is the same:

from isolation → relationship

from treatment → environment

from individual → collective

The Brain Well-Being Model® names the patterns under these shifts, but communities have been practicing them for generations. The work ahead is not to replace what is already working, but to notice it, strengthen it, and design alongside it. When enriched environments are recognized as central rather than peripheral, the question changes from "How do we fix people?" to "How do we build places where people's nervous systems can finally rest, reconnect, and grow?"

A living example of this kind of practice will be explored next through ARTGard and community-based Resilience Studios™—places where play, nature, culture, enriched environments, and nervous-system literacy are woven into everyday life, and where healing is understood as something people do together.

# Chapter 7

# Designing Environments Where the Brain Can Feel Well

Healing environments do not appear by accident. They are shaped by people who decide that survival alone is not enough. If the nervous system adapts to its surroundings, then healing must also involve changing the surroundings themselves. Research on allostatic load, attachment, and polyvagal informed science all point to the same truth. Bodies regulate more easily in environments that are predictable, relational, and culturally honoring. They remain in Guard Mode when spaces are chaotic, isolating, or shaming.

## From Services to Spaces

Services matter. They save lives. Yet services alone cannot carry the full weight of healing when stress is woven into daily life. Communities also need places that feel safe enough to breathe. These are spaces where culture is honored, creativity is welcomed, and support is visible and relational.

In the language of this book, these environments are called Resilience Studios™. They are spaces intentionally designed to support nervous system safety, connection, and possibility. Within the Brain Well Being Model®, Resilience Studios™ are enriched environments where somatic, perceptual, relational, and aspirational awareness can grow together rather than separately.

## Principles of a Brain-Well Environment

Research across attachment, trauma, polyvagal theory, expressive arts, and public health suggests a shared set of conditions that help nervous systems move from Guard Mode toward Healing Mode and, when possible, into early Thrive Mode.

<u>Brain-well environments tend to share these principles:</u>

- **Predictability and rhythm**. Clear openings and closings, consistent routines, and repeated rituals help the nervous system know what is coming next, reducing allostatic load and supporting regulation.

- **Sensory gentleness and choice**. Thoughtful attention to light, sound, clutter, seating, and access to movement allows bodies to downshift and prevents re-triggering, especially for people with trauma histories.

- **Relational warmth and co-regulation**. Warm tone, eye contact offered but not forced, genuine welcome, and repair after conflict create the interpersonal safety attachment and relational neurobiology describe as foundational.

- **Cultural rootedness and representation**. Images, music, language, and practices that reflect the communities present affirm belonging and counteract the erasure that contributes to Guard Mode, particularly for Black, Indigenous, and other communities of color.

- **Opportunities for play, art, and nature**. Access to creative materials, movement, and plants or outdoor space supports regulation and meaning-making beyond words.

- **Visible pathways to support and future orientation**. Clear, non-shaming information about resources, leadership pathways, and next steps nourishes aspirational awareness and counters hopelessness.

These principles are not luxuries. They are practical applications of the Brain Well-Being Model®: ways of designing space so that somatic, perceptual, relational, and aspirational awareness all have room to grow.

## The Resilience Studio™ in Motion

A Resilience Studio™ is not defined by a building. It is defined by conditions: felt safety, consistent relationship, expression without punishment, and access to resources that reduce survival pressure. It can be a room in a school, a corner of a church, a section of a park, a shared garden bed, or a set of practices that travel wherever people gather.

In Guard Mode environments, these studios act as counter-environments. They do not deny the realities outside; they offer repeated experiences of Healing Mode inside, so the nervous system has somewhere to rehearse what it feels like to be regulated, connected, and oriented toward the future.

## ARTGard as Living Practice

ARTGard is one living expression of a Resilience Studio™. It integrates therapeutic art, gardening, play-based regulation, cultural expression, social-emotional learning, and community resource access—not as separate activities, but as one continuous environment of care. Expressive arts and horticultural-therapy research show that creative making and contact with plants can reduce stress, improve mood, and support attention and regulation across ages.

In ARTGard, paint becomes an emotional language. Soil becomes grounding. Rhythm becomes regulation. Presence becomes safety. Because art and gardening are living processes, ARTGard operates as a small ecosystem: people, plants, colors, stories, and supports interact. Somatic awareness is engaged through movement and touch, perceptual awareness through symbol and meaning-making, relational awareness through shared work and co-regulation, and aspirational awareness through imagining what the space—and the community—could grow into over time.

## Community Play Dates and Wellness Labs

What looks like a simple community play date or wellness lab is, in reality, a multi-system intervention: bodies are regulated through movement and rhythm, perceptions soften through art and story, relationships deepen through co-presence, and future orientation is sparked through shared problem-solving and visioning. It is the Brain Well-Being Model® in motion, supported by decades of work in play therapy, expressive arts, trauma-informed care, and community mental health.

Community play dates and wellness labs invite participants to directly experience the four awareness domains, because the brain changes more through state than through information. A drum circle, for example, regulates the body through rhythm (somatic), shifts the story from "I am alone" to "I am part of something" (perceptual), bonds people through shared sound and laughter (relational), and sparks a sense that new ways of being together are possible (aspirational).

## Wellness Kits and Healing Beyond the Event

Wellness kits extend the Resilience Studio™ into homes, shelters, schools, and temporary living spaces. They translate enriched environments into portable form: a small set of materials and practices that invite somatic, perceptual, relational, and aspirational awareness without requiring a clinic or a formal program.

This makes the message unmistakable: healing is not reserved for clinics; regulation is not reserved for professionals. Every kitchen table, bedroom, or shelter cot can become a micro-studio for nervous-system care when people are given tools that respect their realities and rhythms. Wellness kits also align with public-health and community-care approaches that emphasize bringing support to where people live, rather than expecting people to navigate complex systems while in Guard Mode.

## Workforce as Cultural Healing Infrastructure

Healing at scale cannot rely on clinicians alone. It requires a community-rooted workforce—community health workers, doulas, peer specialists, educators, faith leaders, youth leaders—who extend regulation into the places where people live. Public-health and systems-change efforts, including California's CalAIM and community health worker pathways, recognize that sustainable transformation depends on this broader healing workforce.

In this model, these practitioners become cultural healing infrastructure: living extensions of the Resilience Studio™ who carry somatic, perceptual, relational, and aspirational practices into schools, churches, clinics, parks, and homes. They help ensure that the language of Guard Mode, Healing Mode, and Thrive Mode is not confined to therapy offices, but becomes shared nervous-system literacy across families, classrooms, and neighborhoods.

In Part IV, this workforce is explored in more depth as the healing workforce of the future: people and roles that help turn Resilience Studios™ from isolated programs into a way of organizing communities around safety, connection, and shared responsibility.

# Practicing Safety Through F.L.O.W.S.

Knowledge alone does not create healing. Healing begins when understanding becomes experience. The *F.L.O.W.S.* framework offers a simple way to pause, notice, and gently support the nervous system's return toward safety—whether you are in a clinic, classroom, garden, or kitchen.

**F — Feel**

Take a slow breath. Notice your body without trying to change it. Where do you feel tension, warmth, numbness, restlessness? There is no correct sensation—only information.

**L — Listen**

What thoughts are repeating? What emotions are near the surface? Listening does not mean solving. It means allowing the nervous system to be heard.

**O — Open**

Widen attention outward. Notice the space around you. Is there anything—even small—that feels neutral or slightly comforting? Only one percent more possibility is enough to begin.

**W — With**

Who, what, or where helps you feel supported? A person, memory, music, nature, prayer, breath, art, movement. Connection can be human, spiritual, sensory, or environmental.

**S — Step**

Choose one small action that supports well-being in the next hour. A drink of water. A stretch. A text to someone safe. A moment outside. A pause without guilt. Small steps teach the brain: change is possible without danger.

Healing can be relearned as many times as necessary. There is no quota on returning to safety.

# From Guard Mode to Healing Mode: How Regulation Actually Happens

Understanding the nervous system changes how we interpret distress. However, understanding alone does not create healing. Many people can name their triggers and analyze their past, yet their bodies still brace, tighten, and scan for danger. This is not failure. It is biology. The nervous system reorganizes through experience, not through insight alone.

**Regulation Before Reflection**

When the nervous system is in sustained threat detection, the reasoning parts of the brain become less accessible. In this state, asking someone to "think positively" or "make better choices" is neurologically unrealistic. Regulation must come first. Somatic and relational awareness need enough safety so that perceptual and aspirational awareness can open without overwhelm.

**Defining Healing Mode**

Healing Mode is the transitional state between survival activation and sustainable thriving. It is not constant calm. Instead, it is defined by three shifts:

• The body begins to downshift from chronic threat

• Awareness increases without overwhelming the system

• Connection becomes possible again

Within the Brain Well Being Model®, Healing Mode often looks like this. Somatic awareness begins to notice small reductions in tension. Perceptual awareness becomes able to consider more than one interpretation of events. Relational awareness experiments with low risk trust. Aspirational awareness widens just enough to imagine that tomorrow might be slightly different from today.

Healing Mode is fragile at first. Yet once it is experienced, the nervous system remembers the path back.

**The Science of Repetition**

Neuroplasticity depends on consistent experiences that are emotionally safe, sensory rich, and relational. Healing is less like lightning and more like gardening. The brain and body learn through repetition, breath by breath, interaction by interaction, and environment by environment.

This is why enriched environments, Resilience Studios™, and ARTGard spaces matter. They provide many small and safe repetitions of regulation, connection, and possibility rather than waiting for a single breakthrough moment to transform everything. Research in expressive arts and horticultural therapy shows that creative making and contact with plants can reduce stress, improve mood, and support attention and regulation across age groups.

**Why Play Is a Biological Regulator**

Play is not an optional extra. It is a biological regulator. Through play, the nervous system rehearses safety, flexibility, and connection in ways that do not feel like work.

Play activates social engagement, reduces stress chemistry, increases behavioral flexibility, and allows safe experimentation with roles and risks.

For children, this may look like running, drawing, drumming, dancing, building, or digging. For adults, it may appear as movement, art, gardening, games, or creative community gatherings. Adults who rediscover play often say, "I feel like myself again." Not a new self, but the original one that existed before Guard Mode covered it.

**Creative and Sensory Pathways Into Healing Mode**

Because trauma and chronic stress imprint themselves on the body, regulation must include embodied experiences such as art, movement, music, nature, safe touch, and co-regulation. These are not luxuries. They are biological interventions.

Creative and sensory practices help shift Guard Mode toward Healing Mode by:

- Giving the body repetitive and soothing actions, such as brush strokes, kneading clay, watering plants, or walking to a steady rhythm. These support somatic awareness and calming.

- Offering symbols, metaphors, and images that gently expand perceptual awareness beyond rigid "all or nothing" stories.

- Creating shared experiences, such as side by side art tables, garden beds, or drum circles, which deepen relational awareness and support co regulation.

- Sparking small experiences of agency and vision. Moments such as "I made this," "We grew this," or "We finished this together" nourish aspirational awareness.

In this model, art studios, gardens, wellness labs, and community play gatherings are not extracurricular activities. They are structured pathways into Healing Mode.

## The First Signs of Real Healing

Healing rarely begins dramatically. It appears as subtle shifts: reacting less quickly to the same trigger, recovering faster after an argument, falling asleep a bit more easily, feeling one genuine moment of joy, asking for help instead of withdrawing, tolerating stillness for one extra breath. Inside the nervous system, these are enormous.

In Brain Well-Being Index language, these shifts might look like a move from 1 to 2 in somatic awareness (high strain to mixed), from 1 to 2 in perceptual awareness (threat-only to seeing a few options), from 1 to 2 or 3 in relational awareness (guarded to cautiously connected), or from 0 to 1 in aspirational awareness (no future to one small possibility). Each step is a sign that Guard Mode is no longer running the whole story.

## Healing Is Not Linear

People and communities cycle between Guard Mode, Healing Mode, and early experiences of Thriving. The goal is not to stay in any single state forever; the goal is increasing flexibility—the ability to recognize Guard Mode sooner and to return more easily over time.

In practice, this means that setbacks are expected. A community can have a powerful Resilience Studio™ or ARTGard season and still experience moments of collective Guard Mode when violence, loss, or instability return. What changes over time is not the absence of stress, but the presence of pathways: people know more ways to breathe, move, reach out, gather, create, and rest together. The nervous system, individually and collectively, becomes more practiced at finding its way back.

Healing often arrives quietly: a longer breath, a softer shoulder, a moment of laughter that does not feel forced. Once the body experiences even a glimpse of safety, it begins—slowly, carefully, intelligently—to remember how to live.

# Chapter 9

# Measuring What Matters:
## The Brain Well-Being Index

If healing is real, it must be observable. The Brain Well-Being Model® describes how people and communities move from Guard Mode toward Healing Mode and, when possible, into Thrive Mode. The Brain Well-Being Index (BWI) was created to give us a simple way to witness that movement over time—not by counting symptoms alone, but by noticing shifts in regulation, connection, perception, and purpose.

## Why a New Measure Was Needed

Most tools used in mental health and education focus primarily on problems: diagnoses, incidents, absences, suspensions, and crisis calls. These indicators are important, but they reveal very little about whether nervous systems are actually becoming safer, more flexible, and more connected. They do not show whether a child, family, or community can return from Guard Mode more easily than before.

The BWI was developed to measure what traditional tools often overlook. Instead of asking only, "How severe are the symptoms?" it asks a different question: "How is the nervous system moving?" Are bodies settling more often? Are personal stories widening? Are relationships becoming safer? Is aspiration, even in small ways, beginning to return?

In other words, the BWI looks for movement rather than perfection.

For youth and adults living in the digital age, this perspective is especially important. Their nervous systems are not responding only to what happens at home, school, or in the neighborhood. They are also responding to a constant stream of images, alerts, and opinions arriving through phones and screens. This continuous exposure can keep many nervous systems in a low level Guard Mode even when nothing dangerous is happening in the room.

A measurement approach that captures movement back toward regulation, connection, and possibility is therefore not a luxury. It is a necessity.

## What the BWI Measures

The Brain Well-Being Index is built around the four awareness domains introduced earlier in this book. Each domain is scored on a simple scale that reflects state, not identity:

- Somatic regulation. Is the body settling more consistently, even in small ways—sleep improving, tension softening, fewer spikes into overwhelm?

- Perceptual flexibility. Is the story widening? Can the person or community see more than one interpretation, more than one possible outcome, more than one way forward?

- Relational safety. Are people tolerating or initiating connection more often? Is there evidence of co-regulation, repair after conflict, and trusted presence?

- Aspirational agency. Do people feel even a little more capable, needed, and oriented toward the future? Can they name hopes, values, or next steps that feel real?

In practical terms, the BWI asks about things like noticing physical signs of stress, having strategies to calm the body, being able to pause before reacting, feeling supported by at least one person or community, and feeling connected to interests or goals that still matter.

Some versions of the BWI also track joy and play as visible evidence of safety: laughter that is not forced, moments of ease, creative engagement, and shared delight. These are not small details; they are indicators that Guard Mode is not running the whole show.

## Not a Label, Not a Diagnosis

The Brain Well-Being Index is not a diagnostic tool and not a label. It does not tell us who someone is; it only tells us where their nervous system seems to be right now and whether there is movement over time. Scores are snapshots of state, not judgments of character, worth, or potential. The purpose of the BWI is to notice shifts in safety, flexibility, connection, and agency so we can respond with more care—not to categorize people or decide who is "well enough." Movement is the metric, not perfection.

## The Stress-to-State Pathway

The BWI rests on a simple observation about stress and state. Stress does not just "make people upset." It changes how accessible different nervous system states are. Over time, adversity shifts the baseline.

You can think of this as a Stress-to-State Pathway:

1. Adversity layers. Individual adverse experiences combine with community-level stressors such as racism, poverty, violence, displacement, environmental instability, and constant digital exposure.

2. Stress load increases. The body begins to carry more allostatic load—more wear-and-tear from chronic activation.

3. Guard becomes more accessible. The nervous system learns to enter Guard Mode more quickly and more often, even in situations that might be safe.

4. Access to reflection, connection, and purpose decreases. When Guard becomes baseline, it is harder to think clearly, trust others, or feel hopeful about the future.

5. Intentional buffering and regulation are required. Healing does not happen by accident. It requires environments, relationships, and practices that help the system move back toward regulation and connection.

The Brain Well-Being Index was designed to track where someone is along this pathway and, more importantly, whether they are moving. It treats Guard, Healing, and Thrive as states—not identities—and pays attention to how often and how easily a person or community can shift between them.

## The Order of Awareness

Earlier chapters described the four awareness domains as a sequence and a circle. In practice, this sequence also becomes a practical guide for intervention and for what the BWI tracks over time:

- Regulate (Somatic awareness). First, we help bodies feel a little safer: lowering stimulation, offering predictable rhythm, using movement, breath, art, or gardening to settle activation. Regulation precedes reflection.

- Clarify (Perceptual awareness). As the body settles, we can gently widen the story: noticing old survival narratives, introducing alternative explanations, and naming how stress, racism, and digital overload have shaped perception. Reflection precedes connection.

- Connect (Relational awareness). With some regulation and clarity in place, we can strengthen relationships: practicing co-regulation, repair, boundaries, and belonging in families, classrooms, faith spaces, and community programs. Connection precedes purpose.

- Reclaim (Aspirational awareness). As safety stabilizes, people can reclaim agency and future orientation: naming what matters, imagining what could be different, and taking small steps toward shared goals. Purpose grows from this reclaimed agency.

The BWI does not assume that everyone moves through this order in a neat line. Life is messier than that. But it uses this sequence as a compass. Over time, scores that reflect more somatic regulation, more perceptual flexibility, more relational safety, and more aspirational agency tell us that the nervous system—and the community around it—is gaining options.

## Movement, Not Perfection

In Guard Mode, change often feels invisible from the outside. A young person may still struggle in school or at home, even as their nervous system is making important shifts. For this reason, the BWI treats movement as the primary metric.

Examples of meaningful movement might include:

- Somatic regulation shifting from "constant strain" to "mixed"—still stressed, but with more frequent pockets of ease.

- Perceptual awareness shifting from "the worst always happens" to "sometimes things work out differently."

- Relational safety shifting from "I don't trust anyone" to "I have one or two people I can go to."

- Aspirational agency shifting from "I have no future" to "I might be able to finish this program," or "I want to help younger youth not go through what I did."

None of these shifts are dramatic. All of them are biologically and relationally significant. The BWI helps teams see and honor this movement instead of waiting for a complete transformation before acknowledging progress.

## How the BWI Is Used

The Brain Well-Being Index was designed to be usable beyond clinical settings. It can be completed by:

- clinicians and therapists

- educators and school teams

- community health workers and peers

- faith leaders and youth leaders

- caregivers, families, and, in developmentally appropriate ways, youth themselves

It can be used in:

- therapy and counseling sessions

- school wellness centers and classrooms

- ARTGard spaces, wellness labs, and Resilience Studios

- community programs, faith-based initiatives, and outreach events

Sometimes the BWI is completed at the beginning and end of a program cycle. Sometimes it is used more frequently, as a reflective tool during check-ins or case conferences. It can be used by a single practitioner or by a team, as long as everyone shares a common understanding of the domains and the modes. What matters is not who fills it out, but how it is used: as a shared lens for talking about state shifts, and as a guide for adjusting environments and interventions.

The BWI should never be used to label, sort, or gatekeep; its only purpose is to help people and systems see movement and decide how to offer better support.

## Seeds and Leaves: An Arts-Based Way to See BWI

In practice, one of the simplest ways we bring the Brain Well-Being Index to life is through the **Seeds and Leaves** activity, an arts based reflection tool that frames a regulating, play based, or arts based experience. Seeds capture a brief pre activity snapshot of mood and mode. Leaves capture what feels different after engagement. Instead of beginning with scores, participants begin with how they arrive and how they leave.

Participants may complete the BWI before or after the activity, but the Seeds and Leaves drawing itself remains anchored in lived experience. The guiding questions are simple: "How am I arriving?" for seeds, and "What feels possible now?" for leaves. Seeds invite participants to notice their current Guard, Healing, or Thrive state before engagement. Leaves invite them to name outcomes they can sense afterward, such as greater ease in the body, a slightly wider story, a bit more connection, or a small return of hope.

In **ARTGard** settings, Seeds and Leaves are often used with pre printed cards. Participants complete seed cards at the first wellness stations as a baseline state check. They then move through labs designed to support somatic, perceptual, relational, and aspirational awareness. At the end of the experience, participants complete leaf cards reflecting what feels different now and add them to a shared tree. Over time, the tree becomes a visual representation of collective growth.

The act of tending that tree, showing up, adding leaves, protecting it, and pausing to notice it, becomes a simple practice story for how communities can commit to caring for themselves and one another.

For digital age youth in particular, the plant metaphor offers a gentle way to notice BWI related movement without beginning with numbers or clinical language. The detailed steps for implementing Seeds and Leaves in different settings are provided in the appendices. Here it serves as one example of how the Brain Well Being Index can move off the page and into embodied, creative practice.

## A Glimpse of BWI Movement

To bring this into focus, imagine a youth participating in a six-week community wellness lab.

At the beginning, their body is often tense, sleep is irregular, and they are quick to shut down or lash out. Somatic awareness and regulation are low. Their story about life is narrow and threat-based: "Nothing changes," "People like me don't get chances." Relationally, they avoid adults and mistrust peers outside a small circle. Aspirationally, they cannot name anything they are looking forward to.

On their first Seed card, they draw small, dark shapes and write words like "tired," "angry," or "guarded."

After six weeks of art, gardening, movement, and group ritual in a predictable, culturally affirming space, the BWI might show:

- Slightly less constant tension, a bit more ability to settle during activities, and one or two better nights of sleep.

- A softening story: "Sometimes these groups actually help," "Maybe I can finish this semester."

- One or two adults they now identify as "kind of safe," and a willingness to participate in small group work.

- A modest goal named out loud: "I want a job," "I want to help with the younger kids," or "I want to feel less angry all the time."

On their Leaf card, they add a few larger shapes to the page, maybe write words like "calmer," "lighter," or "not alone," and place the card on the shared tree.

On the page, this is a shift of one or two points in each BWI domain. In the nervous system and in the person's life, it is the beginning of a different trajectory. The BWI and Seeds and Leaves together give language and structure to this kind of movement so that practitioners, systems, and communities can see it, support it, and build on it.

## Why This Measure Matters for Equity

In communities shaped by racism, poverty, environmental injustice, historical trauma, and the relentless demands of the digital age, chronic Guard is not an individual weakness. It is a predictable response to conditions. Traditional measures often capture the consequences—suspensions, hospitalizations, arrests, dropout rates—without capturing the safety, creativity, and connection that communities are building in response.

## The Brain Well-Being Index offers a different lens. It asks:

- Where is Guard Mode showing up as a state we can understand and support, rather than a behavior we simply punish?

- Where is Healing Mode already emerging—in barbershops, gardens, faith spaces, youth programs, salons, living rooms, and digital-age "third spaces"—and how can we measure and strengthen those shifts?

- How can we use data to argue not only for more services, but for more environments where nervous systems can rest, reconnect, and reclaim agency?

By tracking somatic, perceptual, relational, and aspirational movement in these contexts, the BWI helps make visible what communities have been doing for generations: surviving, organizing, protecting, and healing in conditions not designed for their thriving.

## Practicing BWI as Shared Language, Not Just a Form

A measure only matters if it changes practice. The Brain Well-Being Index was never meant to be another form buried in an electronic record. It was designed to become a shared language across roles and settings—a simple way for people who care about the same youth, families, and communities to talk about state, safety, and movement in the same terms.

When schools, clinics, community programs, and families all use BWI language, several shifts become possible:

- A teacher can say, "I'm seeing a lot of Guard in this classroom lately," and the school team understands that this is about state and conditions, not just behavior.

- A community health worker can bring a BWI snapshot from ARTGard or a wellness lab into a case conference, helping clinicians see gains in regulation and connection that might not show up in symptom counts yet.

- A parent can be told, "Your child's scores show more somatic ease and a bit more relational trust than last month," and know that progress is happening even if life is still hard.

In this way, BWI becomes less about scoring and more about coordination. It helps teams notice patterns, adjust environments, and choose next steps that align with where a nervous system actually is along the Stress-to-State Pathway.

## How Systems Can Support BWI Use

For systems leaders, the question is not only "Should we adopt this tool?" but also "How do we protect its purpose?" The BWI is most effective when it is used in ways that support people rather than evaluate them in isolation.

The BWI works best when:

- It is used to guide support, not to gatekeep access or punish people for being in Guard Mode.

- It is paired with training in the Brain Well-Being Model® and Guard, Healing, and Thrive language so that scores are interpreted within the proper context.

- It is integrated into existing workflows, such as school meetings, community health worker visits, wellness labs, and supervision, rather than being added as a separate or isolated task.

When used in this way, the BWI can help systems identify where chronic Guard Mode is concentrated and where enriched environments are most needed. It can help track the impact of Resilience Studios™, wellness labs, digital age interventions, and community initiatives over time. It can also strengthen the case for investing in prevention rather than responding only to crises.

In this approach, movement becomes a system wide metric rather than only an individual hope.

## From Numbers Back to Nervous Systems

Ultimately, every BWI score is a story about a nervous system trying to adapt. A low somatic score may reflect years of instability, racism, and digital overload. A small increase in aspirational agency may reflect the impact of one trusted relationship or one predictable space like a garden, a youth room, a salon, or a moderated online community.

If this measure succeeds in its purpose, it will do more than produce data. It will help communities see where Guard is heavy, where Healing is emerging, and where Thrive is already being practiced in small, everyday ways. It will remind us that movement is possible, that states can change, and that when we design for safety and connection, nervous systems respond.

In the next chapter, we turn from framework to landscape, stepping into one specific context—Black Los Angeles—to see Guard Mode in plain sight and to watch how the Brain Well-Being Index helps us witness what is shifting beneath the headlines.

# Chapter 10

# Guard Mode in Plain Sight:
## A Collective Illustration from Black Los Angeles

### Micro-Case Vignette: Before the Numbers

On a Tuesday morning in South Los Angeles, a nine year old girl sits at the kitchen table, already dressed for school.

Her backpack is zipped.

Her shoes are tied.

But she has not moved for twenty minutes.

Her grandmother watches quietly from the stove and recognizes the stillness. Not defiance. Not laziness. Something heavier.

The girl's shoulders are lifted toward her ears. Her breathing is shallow. Her eyes are fixed on nothing in particular.

Outside, a siren passes.

Inside, her body does not change. It has learned not to.

Last month, a fight broke out near the school gate.

Last year, her cousin stopped coming to class.

Most nights, sleep arrives late and leaves early.

When asked what is wrong, she shrugs.

"I'm just tired."

In clinical language, this moment might be called anxiety, hypervigilance, or a trauma response. In school records, it may appear as absenteeism. In public health data, it will disappear into percentages.

Before it becomes any of those things, it is simply a nervous system trying to decide whether the world is safe enough to walk outside the door.

The numbers that follow begin here. This chapter offers a narrative and data informed illustration of Guard Mode at the community level in Black Los Angeles rather than presenting a single formal clinical case. It weaves together population data, local reports, and lived narratives to show how the Brain Well Being Model® and Collective Care in Action® appear within real environments.

## Guard Mode Beyond the Individual

Guard Mode is often discussed as a personal experience, a single nervous system shaped by trauma, instability, or prolonged stress.

Sometimes Guard Mode is not only individual.

Sometimes it is collective.

When entire communities live under chronic exposure to threat through poverty, racism, violence, displacement, medical inequity, and generations of unprocessed grief, protective adaptations can become shared patterns of daily life.

Not because people are broken.

Because protection has been required for too long.

This chapter is intentionally structured as both data and story. It draws on county trend reports, maternal and infant health disparities, and safety and economic indicators, alongside lived narratives from kitchens, schools, churches, barbershops, and salons.

In doing so, it follows the intellectual lineage of writers and thinkers such as James Baldwin, bell hooks, Maya Angelou, Ta-Nehisi Coates, Joy DeGruy, and Resmaa Menakem. Their work reminds us that Black life cannot be reduced to numbers or diagnoses alone. The nervous system, the neighborhood, and the narrative must be held together.

For that reason, the Brain Well Being Model® and Collective Care in Action® are not presented here as abstract frameworks. They are offered as lenses that help make sense of what Black Los Angeles is already surviving and already healing every day.

This chapter examines Guard Mode in plain sight, drawing from lived experience and documented realities within Black communities in Los Angeles.

Not to pathologize.

But to tell the truth clearly enough that healing can finally be designed to fit.

## When Stress Becomes a Community Baseline

Safety, School, and Daily Nervous-System Load

A nervous system cannot think its way out of chronic exposure.

It adapts.

In Los Angeles County, perception of neighborhood safety among Black residents has declined significantly in recent reporting, a shift that reflects more than opinion. Perceived safety directly shapes:

- mental health

- physical health

- sleep

- learning

- civic trust

- long-term life expectancy.

During the same period, chronic absenteeism among Black students rose sharply.

Absenteeism is often framed as a behavioral or academic concern.

Through a nervous-system lens, it may also signal:

- anxiety and hypervigilance

- disrupted sleep

- transportation instability

- school climate stress

- depression or grief

- community threat exposure

- family survival logistics.

These are not moral failures.

They are biological signals.

## Economic Pressure as Biological Exposure

Guard Mode is expensive.

Not metaphorically—physiologically.

Rising poverty rates among Black households in Los Angeles County increase cumulative survival strain:

- housing instability

- food insecurity

- reduced preventive health care

- chronic decision fatigue

- limited opportunity for restorative rest.

When survival logistics dominate daily life, the nervous system learns an unspoken rule:

Relaxation is dangerous.

Because relaxing might mean something falls apart unnoticed.

Guard becomes baseline. The body is rarely allowed to fully exhale. Somatic awareness narrows around tension and readiness. Perceptual awareness begins to favor stories like "I can't afford to trust this," or "If I stop, everything will collapse." Under that strain, relational and aspirational awareness become harder to access—not because people do not care, but because their biology has been recruited into constant watchfulness.

## Violence Against Black Women

Guard Mode Meets Immediate Threat

When disproportionate violence targets a community, Guard Mode becomes rational.

City-level reporting in Los Angeles over more than a decade reveals stark disproportionality in:

- sexual violence

- aggravated assault

- homicide impacting Black women.

This is not abstract trauma theory.

This is daily survival mathematics:

Bodies scanning.

Families adapting.

Communities developing protection strategies that are too often mislabeled as dysfunction by observers outside the threat.

In this context, Guard Mode is not pathology.

It is intelligence.

## Maternal and Family Well-Being

### *When the Body Bears History*

Guard Mode also appears where life should feel safest: pregnancy, birth, and early caregiving.

California data shows:

- Black infants die at more than twice the rate of White infants.

- Black mothers die from pregnancy-related causes at more than four times the rate of White women.

Prenatal depressive symptoms are significantly higher, while access to maternal mental-health care remains lower.

When even life-giving biological processes carry disproportionate threat, the nervous system learns a devastating lesson:

Protection must remain constant, even during moments meant for joy.

Attachment, sleep, and early development are shaped in the shadow of this vigilance. Babies arrive in bodies already carrying echoes of unprocessed stress from previous generations, even as families fight fiercely to offer love and safety.

# Black Los Angeles: Guard Mode and the Everyday Practice of Healing

### Social Story Window: Healing in the Salon Chair

This Social Story Window is shared with permission from loctician and stylist Kyla Eveillard, founder of Naza Locs (@nazalocs), a natural hair studio on Crenshaw in Los Angeles. Her work is deeply rooted in the realities of Black life in LA—traffic and hustle, grief and joy, history and becoming—and her chair has become a quiet healing space for Black men and women who live with daily Guard Mode.

We call this piece a **Social Story "Window"** because that is exactly what it offers: a glimpse into her house, her chair, her salon, and her way of seeing and caring, shared on her own terms. It is not meant to represent every stylist, every salon, or every Black man in Los Angeles. It is a window into one practitioner's lived perspective and the ways Guard Mode and Healing Mode appear in the everyday work of hands, scalp, story, and rest.

Her story appears here for a specific reason. The preceding sections have shown, through data, how persistently suffering appears in Black Los Angeles through neighborhood safety challenges, absenteeism, poverty, violence against Black women, and maternal and infant mortality. This narrative shows that within the very same landscape, rest and self care are actively practiced and protected in everyday Black spaces.

Barbershops and salons in Black Los Angeles function as enriched environments and informal Resilience Studios™. They are trusted places where story, culture, touch, and presence allow nervous systems to settle, even when the structural conditions that keep people in Guard Mode have not yet changed.

This is exactly what the Brain Well Being Model describes as Healing Mode, a fragile and repeating movement from protection toward regulation, connection, and a small reopening of future possibility. It is also what Collective Care in Action® describes as community rooted care: healing that takes place through relationships, culture, and place, not only through formal services.

In the tradition of thinkers such as James Baldwin and Ta-Nehisi Coates, who insist that we acknowledge the full weight of racialized threat, and voices such as bell hooks, Maya Angelou, Joy DeGruy, and Resmaa Menakem, who remind us that love, story, and embodied practice are powerful healing forces, this Social Story Window makes our stance clear.

The model is best understood not through diagrams alone, but through the living, breathing realities of Black Los Angeles.

Guard Mode is not only visible in data.

It is visible in the places where people quietly try to rest from that data every day.

## SOCIAL STORY WINDOW

### Healing in the Salon Chair

*by Kyla Eveillard*

When my clients sit in my chair, I don't just see hair. I see the weight of life resting on tense shoulders. I see the anxieties of the city still clinging to them as they escape the hectic Los

Angeles roads. Often, I look into eyes that are tired in a way sleep alone cannot fix. My clients, Black men and women, show up to the salon wearing their humanity.

For the Black men who sit in my chair, that humanity is often wrapped in armor by the time they walk through the door. They arrive composed, even though the world has already required something from them. Their phones have been ringing, responsibilities have been pulling, and their minds have been calculating, protecting, and providing. Even when they don't say it out loud, I can feel the salon shift into becoming their quiet space, not because it is literally silent, but because it is one of the few places where they don't have to be on guard.

I watch men sink into the chair like their bodies have finally found somewhere to rest. I see them close their eyes at the shampoo bowl and stay there a little longer than necessary. Not asleep—just still. Still in trust. Still in vulnerability. There is something deeply sacred about a Black man allowing someone to touch his head and hair. It is an act of trust that often goes unnamed. As their loctician (and sometimes their unofficial therapist), I lovingly nurture the gift of their truth.

I intentionally curate a safe space, whether that looks like inviting them into genuine check-in conversations, offering room to simply watch their favorite shows, leaving the floor open for them to spill their guts, or playing music that feels like home. It is an honor. It is a privilege. It is a healing realm. And slowly, something shifts and the conversation changes—not always into tears, not always into dramatic confession, but into honesty.

"I've been stressing."

"I don't normally talk to people about this."

"I'm not sure what I should do."

The salon becomes a pause in performance. For an hour or two, they do not have to be the protector, the provider, or the strong one. They can sit. They can be quiet. They can talk. They can exhale.

In a fast and digital world, the salon still matters because it is embodied. It is touch. It is attentiveness. It is presence. It is someone remembering your last appointment and noticing when your energy feels different this time.

I have seen Black men carry grief in their scalps. I have seen stress show up as thinning, tension, and breakage. I have seen fathers, husbands, and sons trying to hold entire worlds together without ever setting the weight down.

In my chair, for a moment, they do not have to hold everything. They can soften. They can breathe. They can simply be human.

## Reading the Moment Through the BWI

In Guard Mode environments, moments like the one in Kyla's chair can be easy to dismiss as "just hair" or "just self-care." They are more than that. They are brief but powerful examples of Healing Mode emerging inside everyday community life. In earlier chapters, the Brain Well-Being Index™ (BWI) was introduced as a simple way to notice state shifts across the four awareness domains—Somatic, Perceptual, Relational, and Aspirational. The example below shows how even one visit to a trusted, culturally rooted space like Naza Locs can create a small but meaningful movement from Guard Mode toward Healing Mode.

## BWI Snapshot

- *Somatic Awareness (SA): 1 → 2*

- High strain → mixed; the body is still carrying stress, but there are brief moments of ease.

- *Perceptual Awareness (PA): 1 → 2*

- Stress-focused → beginning to see options; threat is no longer the only story.

- *Relational Awareness (RA): 1 → 3*

- Guarded → regulating in trusted connection; the client allows co-regulation in a safe relationship.

- *Aspirational Awareness (AA): 0 → 1*

- Little future orientation → a small sense of possibility; the future feels slightly less closed.

## Mode Movement: Guard Mode → Healing Mode (micro- to moderate shift)

In Guard Mode environments, these kinds of shifts may look small on paper, but they are biologically and relationally significant. The body loosens a little. The story widens a little. Trust increases in one specific relationship. The future feels a fraction more possible. This is what Healing Mode looks like in real time—not perfection, but repeated, fragile movements away from constant survival and toward regulation, connection, and hope. These examples demonstrate why the Brain Well-Being Index focuses on state shifts rather than only symptoms: even small movements in somatic, perceptual, relational, and aspirational awareness represent meaningful biological and relational change in Guard Mode environments.

## Purpose of This Collective Illustration

The purpose of this collective illustration is not only to describe suffering; it is to demonstrate how the Brain Well-Being Model® and Collective Care in Action® become real in a specific place. The data show Guard Mode at the community level—heightened allostatic load, shortened life expectancy, disproportionate violence, and maternal risk—while the stories from kitchens, church basements, barbershops, and salons show how somatic, perceptual, relational, and aspirational awareness are already being renegotiated in everyday life.

By holding these side by side, the chapter argues that any serious brain-based model of well-being must be accountable to both: the structural conditions people inherit and the culturally rooted practices through which they rest, resist, and heal.

## The Turn: From Witnessing Survival to Designing Safety

Once Guard Mode is seen clearly—in bodies, schools, birth outcomes, safety data, and the quiet exhaustion inside families—a responsibility emerges.

Not to study survival endlessly.

But to build environments where survival is no longer required.

This is where the book pivots:

- toward workforce pathways that extend regulation into daily life

- toward Resilience Studios™ and wellness labs creating repeated safety

- toward measurement tools like the BWI that document change without shame

- toward culturally intelligent care that names history without recreating harm

Because the future of healing will not be decided only in clinics.

It will be decided in communities that finally receive the safety they were always owed.

## Mirrored Micro-Vignette — The First Shift

Two months later, the same kitchen table.

The girl is still quiet in the mornings.

But today, something small is different.

A paint stained paper sits beside her backpack, left over from an after school art circle held in the church basement down the street.

She had not wanted to go.

Her grandmother brought her anyway.

At first she watched the other children.

Then she picked up a brush.

Blue.

Then yellow.

Then both together.


No one asked questions.

No one rushed her.

Someone hummed softly in the background.


Today, when the siren passes outside, her shoulders still tense, but only for a moment.

Her breath returns a little faster.

Before leaving, she folds the painting carefully and places it in her backpack.

"What's that for?" her grandmother asks.

The girl shrugs, but her voice is quieter now in a different way.

"It just… makes school feel easier."


Nothing dramatic has changed.

The neighborhood is the same.

The stress is still real.

But inside her nervous system, a new possibility has appeared. Small, fragile, and biologically profound.

Safety might be learnable.

And where safety becomes possible, healing has already begun.

# Chapter 11

# The Healing Workforce of the Future

Chapter 10 ended at a kitchen table, a salon chair, and a church basement, three ordinary spaces where Guard Mode was visible and where small movements toward Healing Mode were already taking place. These scenes are not side notes to the mental health system. They are early glimpses of the healing workforce of the future.

That workforce is not made up only of clinicians. It includes community health workers, educators, youth leaders, locticians, barbers, doulas, faith leaders, artists, gardeners, peer mentors, and digital age guides who help nervous systems find their way back from Guard Mode every day.

This chapter explores who this workforce is, what they do at the level of the nervous system, and what conditions they need in order to continue their work without burning out. It also shows how tools such as the Brain Well Being Model®, the Brain Well Being Index (BWI), and Collective Care in Action® can provide shared language and structure for work that many people are already doing intuitively.

## Why We Need a Different Kind of Workforce

Traditional mental health systems were not designed for the world we are living in now. The volume of unprocessed stress, digital age exposure, climate anxiety, racialized violence, economic instability, and intergenerational trauma far exceeds what office based care alone can address.

Clinics are important, but they cannot hold everything. If we rely only on licensed professionals working within billable hours, we will continue to reach too few people, too late, and often only when a crisis has already occurred.

At the same time, countless helpers are already doing healing work without being formally recognized for it. They may be the first person a young person calls when they feel overwhelmed, the adult who sets the emotional tone in a classroom, the barber or stylist whose chair becomes a place where Guard Mode finally softens, or the neighbor who walks a child to school after a difficult night.

These people are not extras in the system. They are primary regulators in their communities. When we recognize them as part of the healing workforce, we can begin to design training, support, and infrastructure that reflect the reality of who is actually helping nervous systems every day.

## From Roles to Functions: What the Healing Workforce Does

The healing workforce of the future is defined less by job title and more by function. Across settings and disciplines, their work clusters around four core functions that mirror the Brain Well-Being Model®:

- Regulate. Help bodies feel safer and more settled in the moment using rhythm, movement, music, breath, touch (when culturally and personally welcome), predictable routines, and sensory-aware environments.

- Clarify. Help people name what is happening to them—linking sensations, emotions, and stress responses to stories that make sense, including the impact of racism, poverty, digital overload, and history.

- Connect. Build and protect relationships where people can be seen, heard, and held without having to perform; strengthen networks of care rather than isolating helpers or clients.

- Reclaim. Support people in naming hopes, values, and small next steps; make it easier for them to contribute, lead, and imagine a future where they matter.

Different roles emphasize different functions. A school social worker may spend more time on clarification and connection, a CHW on regulation and linkage to resources, a loctician on regulation and connection, a youth leader on connection and reclamation of purpose. When they share a common language about Guard, Healing, and Thrive, their efforts begin to work together instead of in parallel.

## Who Belongs in the Healing Workforce of the Future

In this frame, the healing workforce includes:

- Clinical providers. Social workers, psychologists, psychiatrists, counselors, nurses, and primary care providers who integrate Brain Well-Being language into assessment, treatment, and team collaboration.

- Community health workers and promotoras. Trusted community members who bridge homes, clinics, schools, and systems; they often see state shifts long before anyone else.

- Educators and school staff. Teachers, administrators, school counselors, after-school leaders, and classified staff who set daily nervous-system climate in classrooms and hallways.

- Youth and peer leaders. Young adults with lived experience who support peers in navigating systems, digital landscapes, and transitions.

- Cultural healers and creative practitioners. Locticians, barbers, artists, musicians, gardeners, movement teachers, and storytellers whose spaces function as informal Resilience Studios™.

- Birth and family support. Doulas, lactation consultants, parent partners, early childhood educators, and home visitors who influence the earliest patterns of safety and connection.

- Faith and spiritual leaders. Pastors, imams, priests, lay leaders, and spiritual elders whose communities often serve as first responders to grief, crisis, and hope.

Many of these roles already exist. What is new is the recognition that they are all working on the same nervous-system project, and that they deserve training, tools, and structures that reflect that truth.

# Resilience Studios™ and Wellness Labs as Workplaces

In earlier chapters, Resilience Studios™ and wellness labs were introduced as designed environments where nervous systems can reliably find cues of safety, connection, and possibility. They are also prototypes for how the healing workforce of the future should experience their own workplaces. A Resilience Studio™ is not only a place where participants regulate; it is a place where staff are not constantly pulled back into Guard by chaos, overload, and isolation.

## What Is a Resilience Studio™?

In this book, a **Resilience Studio™** is a deliberately designed space, physical or hybrid, where nervous systems can reliably encounter cues of safety, connection, and possibility. It is not a single program or curriculum. It is an environment where somatic, perceptual, relational, and aspirational awareness are intentionally supported through rhythm, creative practice, culture, and co-regulation.

Resilience Studios™ can exist within schools, clinics, faith communities, community centers, or ARTGard sites. They are typically supported by a mix of clinical and non clinical healers who share a common language about Guard Mode, Healing Mode, and Thrive Mode.

In practical terms, this means creating spaces that are predictable, sensory aware, and grounded in relationship. It may include clearly marked rhythms for opening and closing the day, intentional transitions between high energy and quiet activities, and visual cues, such as the ARTGard Seeds and Leaves tree, that remind everyone that growth is happening even when progress feels slow.

It also means building co-regulation time into the structure of the workday. This might include brief grounding practices during shift transitions, protected debrief circles after difficult days, and leadership that treats staff regulation as part of the work rather than a distraction from it.

When Resilience Studios™ and wellness labs are designed in this way, they become living expressions of the Brain Well Being Model®. Somatic safety is reflected in the physical environment. Perceptual clarity appears in how the work is framed. Relational reliability develops within teams. Aspirational energy is reflected in the shared goals people pursue together.

In these environments, staff and community members learn side by side that it is possible to work, learn, and heal in spaces where Guard Mode is acknowledged but not in control. Over time, these sites can become training grounds, demonstrating to schools, clinics, and agencies what it looks like to organize daily operations around nervous system health rather than productivity alone.

## Training Pathways and Role Maps

Recognizing a broader healing workforce is only the first step. The next step is building training pathways that honor different starting points and lived experience. A loctician, a community health worker, a teacher, and an MSW intern do not need identical training, but they do need a shared map. Role maps help clarify what each role is already doing in terms of regulation, clarification, connection, and reclamation, and what additional skills or supports could deepen that work.

For example, community health workers often begin with strong relational and cultural skills. A training pathway for them might focus on basic nervous system literacy, including the language of Guard Mode, Healing Mode, and Thrive Mode. It might also introduce simple somatic and perceptual tools that can be safely shared with others, along with ways to use the Brain Well Being Index and the Seeds and Leaves activity as engagement tools rather than formal assessments.

Educators might receive training on recognizing Guard Mode patterns in the classroom, practicing trauma aware approaches to discipline, creating co-regulation routines, and collaborating with community health workers and clinicians using Brain Well Being language instead of relying only on academic or behavioral labels.

Creative and cultural practitioners, including locticians, barbers, artists, and gardeners, can be offered short and accessible modules that recognize the healing work they are already doing. These modules can add just enough structure to support them while protecting their boundaries. This may include guidance on maintaining clear limits so they do not become isolated informal therapists, warm handoff processes to clinical partners when additional care is needed, and simple reflection tools that help them recognize their own impact without carrying the work alone.

Clinical providers can also be trained to view these practitioners as colleagues within a wider healing network rather than as non professional extras. In this approach, care plans can be created collaboratively and may include community spaces such as salons, gardens, or creative studios as legitimate sites for regulation and connection.

Over time, these pathways can develop into tiered training structures. Introductory foundations may be available to anyone participating in the healing workforce. Intermediate practice modules may support those leading groups or wellness labs. Advanced training may prepare leaders to guide Resilience Studios™, supervise teams, or integrate Brain Well Being metrics into system design.

The goal is not to turn everyone into the same kind of helper. The goal is to give each role a clear and dignified place within a shared ecosystem of care.

## Digital-Age Skills for the Healing Workforce

The healing workforce of the future must be fluent in the realities of digital-age stress. Youth and adults are carrying Guard in their pockets: notifications that never stop, crisis headlines, comparison culture, algorithm-driven content, and constant invitations to perform or be seen. Helpers who ignore this landscape risk missing one of the primary sources of nervous-system activation in daily life.

Digital-age skills do not require becoming a tech expert. They begin with understanding how online environments can act as both a threat and resource for the nervous system. This means noticing how doomscrolling, cyberbullying, viral violence videos, or constant group-chat drama can keep youth in low-grade Guard even in otherwise safe spaces, and how moderated online communities, affirming content, and digital creative expression can sometimes offer real moments of Healing Mode—connection, laughter, solidarity, and inspiration.

For the healing workforce, core digital-age skills include:

- asking gentle, non-shaming questions about how phones, games, and social media actually feel in the body and mind

- helping youth and adults link certain digital patterns to Guard, Healing, or Thrive, using the same language they use for offline environments

- co-creating realistic boundaries, rituals, and micro-pauses around devices (for example, grounding before opening certain apps, or using Seeds and Leaves as a quick "before/after" check for digital spaces just as in physical labs)

- advocating with systems—schools, platforms, program funders—for digital practices and policies that reduce constant threat signals and protect attention, sleep, and connection

In this way, digital-age competence becomes a standard part of the healing workforce's toolkit, not a separate specialty. Whether a helper is in a clinic, a classroom, a salon, a youth room, or a garden, they can recognize that nervous systems are moving between physical and digital environments all day long and can design their support accordingly. This keeps the Brain Well-Being Model® honest about the world youth and families actually live in, and prepares the workforce to meet them there with both compassion and practical tools.

## A Day in the Life of a Community Health Worker in a Resilience Studio™

To see the healing workforce of the future in motion, imagine a community health worker named Jordan working in a neighborhood Resilience Studio™ connected to a school and an ARTGard site. Jordan is not a therapist. They are a bridge: between families and systems, between data and story, between Guard Mode and the possibility of Healing Mode.

Jordan's day begins before participants arrive. They walk through the studio, checking the sensory environment. The lights are softened. Music plays quietly. Art materials are stocked. Seeds and Leaves cards are set out at the opening station. The Brain Well-Being Index clipboard is ready for those due for a check-in.

Before the day begins, Jordan pauses for two minutes. They feel their feet on the ground, notice their breathing, and say to a colleague, "I'm a little Guard this morning. Let's keep an eye on each other." Before supporting anyone else's nervous system, they acknowledge their own.

As youth and caregivers begin to arrive, Jordan greets each person by name. At the Seeds station, they invite a simple pre-check.

"Pick a seed that shows how you're arriving today, your mood, your mode."

Some youth scribble quickly. Others pause and write words like "tired," "mad," or "numb." Jordan does not force conversation. Their presence becomes the first intervention: steady, predictable, and warm.

When a caregiver appears particularly strained, Jordan quietly offers, "Do you want to sit for a minute before you leave? We have tea in the corner." The work here is somatic and relational long before any form is completed.

By midmorning, Jordan meets with a small group of middle school students referred for behavior concerns. Instead of beginning with rules, they begin with bodies and stories. Together they notice where Guard Mode appears during the week: in the classroom when a teacher raises their voice, on the bus when a fight breaks out, online when a group chat turns hostile.

Jordan introduces the Brain Well-Being Model® in simple language and uses a blank Brain Well-Being Index form as a conversation guide rather than a test.

"When your stress is high, how is your sleep? Who do you talk to? Is there anything, even small, that helps you feel a little better?"

Youth fill out items with Jordan's support. Checkboxes become a shared language.

Later in the afternoon, Jordan joins a care coordination meeting with a school social worker, a teacher, and a caregiver. Instead of reporting only attendance issues or noncompliance, Jordan shares a short Brain Well-Being Index summary along with observations from the studio.

"In the last six weeks, their somatic and relational scores have moved up a point. They're sleeping a little better and using the art table to calm down. We're still seeing low hope, so maybe the next step is building something small they can look forward to at school."

The conversation shifts. The team begins speaking in terms of Guard Mode, Healing Mode, and Thrive Mode rather than focusing only on punishment or praise.

Between meetings, Jordan joins a brief staff grounding circle. For five minutes, team members pause to name their current mode, share one thing that feels heavy, and one thing that brought a hint of joy.

This is Collective Care in Action® within the workforce itself. The same principles offered to youth—regulation, reflection, connection, and purpose—are practiced among staff so that helpers do not become invisible in the story of healing.

At the end of the day, youth complete Leaf cards at the closing station. Jordan invites them to notice any shifts.

"What feels even a little different after being here today?"

Some leaves say "calmer," "heard," or "less mad." Others say "no change." All responses are welcome.

Jordan helps tape the leaves onto the growing tree and pauses to look at it with a colleague. The way they care for the tree, showing up, tending it, making space for every leaf, becomes a reflection of how they care for themselves and their community.

Jordan leaves the studio tired but not emptied. Their work has been to translate the Brain Well-Being Model® into everyday gestures: a greeting at the door, a question that opens a story, a Brain Well-Being Index score used to advocate for support rather than restriction, a five minute pause that prevents a colleague from burning out.

They are one example of the healing workforce of the future: rooted in community, fluent in nervous systems, and supported by structures that remember helpers are human too.

As this chapter closes, the healing workforce of the future stands not as an abstract idea, but as a real set of people already holding nervous systems in kitchens, classrooms, clinics, salons, churches, gardens, and digital spaces. Their daily work shows that Guard is not the end of the story when environments are designed to support regulation, connection, and shared purpose. Chapter 12 turns toward the larger question these workers make unavoidable: if this is what becomes possible inside a Resilience Studio™ or wellness lab, what would it mean to design whole neighborhoods, schools, systems, and policies so that thriving is not rare, but normal?

# Designing a World Where Thriving Is Normal

The previous chapter introduced the healing workforce of the future: a web of clinicians, community health workers, educators, youth leaders, doulas, locticians, barbers, artists, gardeners, faith leaders, and digital-age guides who help nervous systems move from Guard toward Healing and Thrive in everyday spaces. Their work lives in Resilience Studios™ and wellness labs, in ARTGard sites and classrooms, in salons and sanctuaries, in youth rooms and on group chats.

This chapter widens the lens. It asks a simple but demanding question: What would it take to design our environments so that thriving is not an exception, but the expected condition? Instead of asking individual children and families to be endlessly resilient inside systems organized around Guard, we begin asking systems themselves to become more regulating, relational, and humane.

## From Individual Change to Environmental Design

Traditional mental health conversations often focus on individual change: new coping skills, insight, behavior plans, or treatment plans. These are important, but they are not enough. When the environment's people return to remain noisy, unpredictable, isolating, or unsafe, Guard Mode quickly reclaims whatever ground was gained in an office or group. Healing becomes a temporary state rather than a supported way of life.

The Brain Well-Being Model® invites a different starting point: design environments that ask less of the nervous system. This means:

- fewer surprises and more predictable rhythms

- fewer shaming interactions and more repair

- fewer isolated helpers and more shared responsibility

- fewer crisis-only responses and more preventative structures

When somatic, perceptual, relational, and aspirational awareness are supported by design—not only by individual effort—Guard no longer has to be the default. People still experience stress and pain, but they do so inside systems that help them move back toward safety, connection, and purpose instead of keeping them stuck.


## Principles for Thriving-Centered Design

Across settings, four design principles emerge from the Brain Well-Being Model® and Collective Care in Action®:

1. Regulate the environment.

2. Design spaces, routines, and policies that lower baseline threat signals rather than increase them.

3. Make safety legible.

4. Ensure people can see, hear, and feel where safety lives: clear processes, transparent communication, consistent follow-through.

5. Center relationships, not just roles.

6. Build structures that protect time and space for connection, co-regulation, and repair.

7. Protect hope and possibility.

8. Embed pathways for voice, choice, creativity, and contribution so that aspirational awareness is nourished, not eroded.

These principles are not extra to the work; they are the work. They take shape differently in schools, clinics, faith spaces, public systems, and digital platforms, but the nervous system questions they answer are the same: Am I safe? Do I matter here? Is there a future for me in this place?

## Designing Schools as Everyday Resilience Studios™

Schools are one of the most powerful—and often underutilized—sites for thriving-centered design. For many children and youth, school is where they spend most of their waking hours, where their bodies and stories are read (or misread) by adults, and where Guard patterns are either reinforced or gently interrupted.

Designing a school as an everyday Resilience Studio™ does not mean turning every classroom into a therapy group. It means aligning daily structures with what we already know about nervous systems:

- Somatic design. Classrooms with predictable routines for arrival and transition, accessible regulation corners or "calm stations," attention to noise and light, and brief whole-class regulation moments woven into the day.

- Perceptual design. Shared language about Guard, Healing, and Thrive; visuals that reflect students' cultures and strengths; explicit teaching that "behavior is communication," not character.

- Relational design. Relationship-first policies: advisory periods or homerooms where at least one adult knows each student well; discipline models that prioritize repair over exclusion; routines for checking in, not just checking work.

- Aspirational design. Regular opportunities for students to lead, create, mentor younger peers, co-design projects, and see their futures reflected in curricula, guests, and partnerships.

In these schools, the healing workforce of the future is visible: teachers who understand Guard patterns, CHWs who bridge home and school, youth leaders who facilitate peer circles, and Resilience Studio™ or wellness lab staff who hold space for regulation, reflection, and ARTGard practice. The BWI becomes one of several tools that help teams notice when students, families, and staff are moving toward more sustainable patterns of well-being.

# Clinics and Agencies as Resilience Studios™ for Helpers

Health and social service agencies often carry high allostatic load themselves. Staff experience constant exposure to crisis, heavy caseloads, administrative pressure, and limited time for integration or rest. In such environments, Guard Mode is not only a client phenomenon; it becomes a workplace norm.

Designing clinics and agencies as Resilience Studios™ for helpers means rethinking both culture and structure:

- embedding brief grounding and check-in practices into staff meetings and shift changes

- designing physical spaces with quiet rooms, natural elements, and art that reflects staff and community

- setting caseload expectations that acknowledge reality rather than romanticizing endless capacity

- normalizing supervision and consultation that attend to nervous-system health, not just compliance and documentation

When agencies adopt Brain Well-Being language internally, staff can say things like, "Our team is in collective Guard this week; what can we pause or simplify?" This turns self-awareness into organizational practice. Over time, agencies that care for their own people in this way are better able to offer consistent, relational, and aspirational care to the communities they serve.

## Faith Spaces, Gardens, and Cultural Hubs as Anchors

Many communities already have places that function as informal Resilience Studios™: churches and mosques, community gardens, cultural centers, arts venues, and recreation centers. These spaces carry memory, ritual, and relationship that no new program can quickly replicate.

Thriving-centered design in these settings begins with honoring what is already working—music, food, movement, prayer, storytelling, mutual aid—and then adding light scaffolding from the Brain Well-Being Model®:

- Naming existing practices (choirs, prayer circles, youth groups, gardening days) as regulation and connection work, not just "activities."

- Offering gentle training on Guard, Healing, and Thrive to lay leaders, choir directors, youth volunteers, and elders.

- Integrating simple tools—check-ins, Seeds and Leaves reflections, BWI snapshots for interested participants—without medicalizing the space.

These hubs often become anchors in a local ecosystem of care. They can host Resilience Studios™ and wellness labs, partner with schools and clinics, and serve as trusted sites for training the broader healing workforce in culturally rooted ways.

## Digital Spaces as Part of the Environment

Today's environment is not only physical. Youth and adults live in overlapping physical and digital worlds, and both shape nervous-system state. Designing for thriving therefore includes digital spaces: school platforms, messaging apps, social media, games, and online communities.

A thriving-centered approach to digital design might include:

- co-creating guidelines with youth about which online spaces feel like Guard, which feel like Healing, and which rarely support Thrive

- designing moderated group spaces where youth can connect around art, gardening, music, and shared interests with clear safety practices

- using ARTGard, Seeds and Leaves, or similar tools to help youth reflect on how certain digital experiences impact their bodies and stories

- partnering with technologists, youth, and community leaders to advocate for platform practices that reduce constant exposure to violence, harassment, and surveillance

When digital design is included in the conversation about the environment, the healing workforce of the future is better equipped to support youth where they actually live: in blended worlds that can either amplify Guard or create surprising pockets of connection and possibility.

## Using the BWI to Inform Design, Not Police It

The Brain Well-Being Index appears again in this chapter, not as an individual scorecard, but as a design mirror. When used thoughtfully, BWI patterns can help teams ask better questions about environments:

- If somatic scores are consistently low across a program, what about the physical space, schedule, or workload may be keeping bodies in Guard?

- If relational scores are low for staff, what does that reveal about supervision, team culture, or isolation?

- If aspirational scores are low for youth in a particular setting, what might need to change about voice, choice, representation, or pathways to leadership?

In this way, the BWI becomes a feedback tool for systems as much as for individuals. It helps leaders see where their environments are quietly pulling people back into survival and where design changes might create more consistent access to Healing and Thrive. Importantly, these data are used to advocate for support and redesign, not to shame staff or communities for the conditions they did not create.

## From Pilot Spaces to a Culture of Thriving

Resilience Studios™, wellness labs, ARTGard sites, and model schools or agencies are important, but they are not the end point. If thriving is to become normal, not rare, these spaces must seed a broader cultural shift. That shift looks like:

- public language about Guard, Healing, and Thrive that shows up in policy documents, training materials, funding announcements, and community meetings

- cross-sector partnerships where schools, clinics, faith organizations, youth groups, and cultural hubs design together instead of in isolation

- investments in the healing workforce of the future as a core part of public infrastructure, not as a short-term grant project

- accountability structures that ask not only, "Did we provide services?" but "Did our environments become more regulating, relational, and hopeful over time?"

In this emerging culture, thriving is not treated as a luxury outcome for a few. It is understood as a baseline responsibility of systems that claim to care for children, families, and communities.

## Looking Ahead: From Design to Practice

Designing a world where thriving is normal requires imagination, courage, and repetition. It means choosing, again and again, to organize around nervous systems instead of convenience, efficiency, or control. It asks leaders to become students of Guard, Healing, and Thrive in their own bodies and institutions, and to invite communities into that learning.

The chapters that follow turn more explicitly toward practice: how individuals, teams, and communities can live these designs in real time, how healing can shift from theory to daily habit, and how Guard Mode can become not a permanent identity, but a place we know how to move through—together.

# Chapter 13

# From Individual Healing to Collective Transformation

### Resilience Is Not Bootstraps

Healing rarely ends with one person.

A child who begins to feel safe changes the rhythm of a classroom.

A parent who learns regulation changes the tone of a home.

A clinician who understands nervous system safety changes the culture of care.

When enough of these shifts gather in the same place, something larger begins to move. Communities begin to organize around possibility rather than survival.

This is the quiet turning point where personal healing becomes public health.

At that point, the word **resilience** requires new honesty.

Resilience is often praised, especially in communities that have survived more than any nervous system was meant to carry. But what we often call resilience is something else: adaptation under threat.

Not individual grit.
Not exceptionalism.
Adaptation.

Human bodies are remarkably adaptive. They can function under pressure, organize around danger, and perform with excellence while carrying fear, grief, and exhaustion.

Yet the nervous system pays for what society celebrates.

For many communities, particularly Black communities, immigrant families, working class households, and those living with chronic poverty, that cost becomes cumulative, generational, and often invisible to those who do not carry it.

Resilience without recovery becomes harm.

Overfunctioning is not sustainability.

And what we often praise as strength may actually reflect chronic Guard Mode.

## Why Individual Change Alone Cannot Carry the Future

For decades, modern mental health systems have focused primarily on the individual: individual diagnoses, individual therapy, individual coping strategies, and the expectation that wellness is primarily a personal responsibility.

These approaches matter. They save lives every day.

But they are incomplete.

Many of the forces pushing nervous systems into Guard Mode are not individual problems at all. They are structural conditions: poverty, racism, housing instability, community violence, educational inequity, environmental stress, and historical trauma carried across generations.

No breathing exercise alone can resolve structural instability.

No worksheet alone can undo collective loss.

And no single clinician can regulate a community living in chronic uncertainty.

Healing must therefore expand from inside the person to around the person.

## The Physiology of Overfunctioning

Chronic stress leaves a signature in the body.

Stress hormones such as cortisol and adrenaline remain elevated. Inflammation rises. Sleep becomes shallow or irregular. Digestion becomes erratic. Immune function weakens, and the brain systems responsible for planning, memory, and emotional regulation begin to struggle.

Over time, this produces what researchers call **allostatic load**—the cumulative wear and tear that occurs when stress is constant and recovery is rare.

Allostatic load is not theoretical. It is measurable.

And it is deadly.

Higher allostatic load is associated with increased rates of heart disease, hypertension, autoimmune conditions, diabetes, stroke, and early mortality. Communities living under chronic threat carry the highest levels of this physiological burden.

Not by accident.

By design.

## Poverty as a Chronic Stress Environment

Poverty is often described as a lack of money, but biologically it functions as a constant threat environment.

Unpredictable housing, food insecurity, noise, unsafe streets, unstable childcare, discrimination in schools, workplace stress, and limited access to medical care all interrupt the nervous system's ability to rest and repair. Over time these conditions shape how the brain develops.

Children growing up in poverty often show higher baseline stress levels, changes in fear regulation systems, and fewer opportunities for the enriched environments that support curiosity, exploration, and learning. These are precisely the conditions that keep Guard Mode active.

This is not a character flaw.

It is a physiological response to deprivation.

And racial inequities ensure that poverty is not distributed equally.

## The Inequities of Stress

Across the United States, and in places such as Los Angeles County, Black communities experience disproportionate rates of hypertension, maternal and infant mortality, chronic illness, and stress-related disease.

These disparities are often presented as statistics, but statistics alone can feel distant. What they represent biologically is generations of nervous systems forced to remain vigilant for survival.

Guard Mode, in this context, is not pathology.

It is inheritance shaped by environment.

Any model of healing that ignores this reality risks treating symptoms while leaving causes untouched.

## When Strength Becomes Armor

In many communities, overfunctioning becomes a survival strategy.

Children grow up too quickly, becoming emotional caretakers for adults around them. Parents keep moving long after exhaustion has set in. Professionals work twice as hard to be seen as equal. Students excel academically while quietly dissociating. Caregivers never rest. Leaders hold entire systems together without support.

These patterns are praised in public and endured in private.

But overfunctioning is not resilience. It is hypervigilance disguised as competence.

When recovery is unavailable, the nervous system begins to lose the ability to distinguish between "I must" and "I can."

Rest begins to feel shameful.

Stillness begins to feel dangerous.

Boundaries begin to feel selfish.

Slowing down triggers anxiety.

The body forgets how to exist without constant effort.

This is the hidden cost of resilience in a culture that refuses to remove threats.

## Overfunctioning in the Digital Age

Digital life intensifies this pattern.

Social media accelerates comparison. News cycles amplify fear. Algorithms reward outrage and urgency. Notifications fragment attention and keep the nervous system in a state of constant responsiveness.

Young people are growing up in an environment that quietly trains the brain to remain alert at all times: perform, respond, keep up, do not miss out, do not fall behind.

Digital Guard Mode is real.

And it compounds racial, economic, and generational stress.

Digital-age overwhelm is not a youth problem alone.

It is a collective nervous-system problem.

## The Public Health Lens: When Biology Meets Environment

Public health research has long demonstrated a simple but profound truth: where people live shapes how long they live.

Neighborhood safety, access to food, housing stability, exposure to violence, educational opportunity, and structural racism all influence stress physiology, chronic disease rates, maternal and infant outcomes, mental health risk, and life expectancy itself.

In communities exposed to sustained adversity, Guard Mode becomes a form of adaptation. Yet adaptation to chronic threat carries a biological cost. Inflammation rises, cardiovascular strain increases, sleep becomes disrupted, emotional vigilance intensifies, and life expectancy shortens.

Seen through this lens, mental health is not only psychological. It is ecological.

Healing cannot remain confined to therapy rooms if the environments outside those rooms continue producing harm faster than treatment can repair it.

## Collective Efficacy: The Missing Mechanism of Hope

Social science offers a powerful concept with enormous implications for healing: **collective efficacy**.

Collective efficacy refers to the shared belief within a community that people can act together to create safety, stability, and change.

Where collective efficacy is strong, several patterns tend to appear:

- Violence decreases.

- Youth engagement rises.

- Health outcomes improve.

- Community resilience strengthens.

- Hope becomes visible in everyday behavior.

The nervous system responds to these conditions.

When people see neighbors supporting neighbors, trusted adults showing up consistently, safe places to gather, shared rituals of care, and visible pathways toward the future, the brain receives new evidence.

We are not alone.

Safety might be possible here.

Gradually, Guard Mode begins to loosen its grip.

## From Disparity to Design: Where Collective Care Enters

If environments shape distress, they can also be redesigned to support regulation.

This is the central premise of ***Collective Care in Action®.***

Not kindness alone.

Not services alone.

Collective care emerges through the intentional design of environments, relationships, and systems that make safety and belonging more biologically likely.

We begin to see this when communities create spaces and rhythms that nurture regulation. Safe gathering places appear. Cultural rituals are honored. Wellness supports become accessible. Trusted relational networks develop. Opportunities for creativity, play, and contribution become part of everyday life. Bridges begin to form between community life and health systems.

These conditions do more than comfort people. They shift stress physiology at a population level.

This is not metaphor.

It is public health intervention.

## California as an Emerging Laboratory of Collective Healing

In recent years, California has begun investing in community based mental health infrastructure that reflects this shift.

Community health workers are being integrated into care teams. Doula services are expanding in response to birth equity needs. Schools are receiving funding for wellness initiatives and prevention programs. Medi Cal transformation through CalAIM has begun recognizing social determinants of health as legitimate health care needs.

These developments signal something important.

Health systems are beginning to understand that regulation cannot be prescribed if environments remain unsafe.

The work remains imperfect and incomplete. Yet these changes represent an early blueprint for translating collective care into policy, workforce design, and funding priorities.

In this sense, California becomes more than a location. It becomes a case study in progress. Evidence that large scale healing design is possible.

## Youth, Environment, and the Long Arc of Prevention

Perhaps the most powerful implications of collective transformation appear in the lives of children.

When young people grow inside environments that provide safety, play, trusted relationships, cultural belonging, opportunities for leadership, and visible hope, their nervous systems organize differently.

Executive functioning strengthens. Emotional regulation becomes more stable. Learning capacity expands. Future orientation becomes possible.

Prevention, in this light, is not simply a program.

It is an environmental condition.

And Collective Care in Action® becomes prevention made visible.

## What Collective Transformation Truly Means

Collective transformation rarely happens quickly. It is not perfect, and it is never finished.

It unfolds through regulated relationships repeated over time, environments organized around belonging, cultures honored as sources of healing, prevention funded alongside treatment, and communities trusted as co designers of health.

This work moves slowly.

Yet it is the only scale of work capable of meeting the scale of suffering we face.

## Reflection and Practice: Coming Home from Overfunctioning

Take a moment to reflect on the following questions:

- Where did you learn that rest was unsafe or undeserved?

- What emotions arise when you imagine slowing down?

- Which parts of your identity have become tied to performance or excellence?

- How have poverty, racism, or instability shaped your stress patterns?

- Whose needs did you learn to prioritize over your own?

## Practice Invitations

- **Micro-Rest Ritual:** Take two minutes for breathing, stretching, or sensory grounding.

- **Saying No Practice:** Decline one nonessential task this week.

- **Reclaim a Boundary:** Choose one hour where you are intentionally unavailable.

- **Name Your Armor:** Write down one "strength" that may actually be overfunctioning.

- **Create a Recovery Cue:** Choose a candle, song, or movement that signals safety to your body.

Resilience is not the ability to endure more.

It is the set of conditions that allow you to need less protection.

## The Bridge Forward

Individual healing matters deeply. Nothing in collective care replaces it.

But individual healing alone cannot carry the future.

The next chapters move further into this widening circle. They explore daily practices that help Guard Mode loosen its grip, pathways for intergenerational restoration, and the workforce and system designs capable of sustaining care across entire communities.

The question at the center of this work is no longer only:

How do we help one person heal?

The deeper question becomes:

How do we build a world where healing becomes more likely for everyone?

Once that question is asked honestly, it begins to change everything that must come next.

# Chapter 14

# When Healing Becomes Practice

The last chapter named a hard truth: individual healing, on its own, cannot carry the weight of structural stress, historical trauma, and digital age overwhelm. It also named a hopeful counterpoint. When enough bodies, homes, classrooms, and systems begin to shift, Guard Mode loosens its grip not just for one person but for whole communities. Collective transformation, however, does not arrive all at once. It arrives as practice.

Practice is what turns insight into habit and habit into culture. It is the difference between knowing that somatic awareness matters and actually checking in with your body before answering one more email or responding to one more crisis. Practice is how a model leaves the page and enters kitchens, Resilience Studios™, staff meetings, and school hallways.

To see what this looks like in real life, we return to two places where the Brain Well-Being Model® and Collective Care in Action® are already alive: a family kitchen and a neighborhood Resilience Studio™. Neither setting is perfect, and both are learning in real time. Together they offer a glimpse of what happens when healing stops being an idea and becomes part of the daily rhythm.

## A Caregiver's Week When Healing Becomes Practice

On Monday morning, Maya wakes before her children. For years, mornings have meant rushing: lunches half made, emails already pinging, everyone's shoulders tense before the day even begins. Lately, something different has been happening. Instead of grabbing her phone first, Maya sits at the small kitchen table for three minutes with a cup of tea, feet on the floor and one hand resting on her chest. She does not call it somatic awareness. She simply notices the signals of her body: her jaw, her breath, her shoulders.

"Guard," she whispers to herself, naming the tightness without judgment. Then she takes five slower breaths and asks, "What do I need to make this morning just a little softer?" Today the answer is simple. She turns on music instead of the news.

When her son and daughter wander in, sleepy and hungry, they find the music playing quietly and a stack of Seeds cards on the table. Maya has started using them as a family check in, not every day but often enough that it has begun to feel like a rhythm. "Pick a seed that shows how you're arriving," she says, sliding the cards toward them.

Her daughter chooses a messy swirl and laughs. "My brain is like this." Her son picks a small dark circle and mutters, "Tired." Maya chooses one too. "Mine's a little jagged today," she admits. "I didn't sleep well." There is no lecture and no forced sharing. Just three people glancing at one another's cards and understanding more than they say out loud.

Midweek, after a difficult phone call with a school administrator about her son's behavior, Maya feels her body shoot back into old patterns. Her heart races, her stomach tightens, and her thoughts begin spinning: They think I'm a bad mother. He's going to get pushed out. She notices her hands gripping the steering wheel. In the past she would have driven home on autopilot, fury and shame braided together.

Today she pulls over a block away, places both feet firmly on the floor of the car, and names what is happening. Her whole body is in Guard. She opens the glove compartment where she has tucked a small F.L.O.W.S. card from the Resilience Studio™: Feel, Locate, Open, Witness, Shift. Slowly she steps through it. She feels the heat in her face, locates the tightness in her chest, and opens a little space with three steady breaths. She witnesses the story forming in her mind, "They're against us," without arguing with it. Then she shifts one small thing she can control. She texts a trusted community health worker at the school and asks if they can talk briefly before the next meeting. In that moment she remembers something important: she is not alone in this.

By Thursday evening exhaustion begins to settle in. The week has been full of work, elder care, school emails, and bills. Old scripts start pulling at her: keep going, hold it all together, collapse later. Instead, Maya looks at the Seeds cards taped to the refrigerator. Some are hers and some belong to her children. She remembers a reflection she wrote during a community workshop: My worth is not measured by how much I endure.

She calls the kids into the living room, pulls out blank Leaves cards, and suggests a ten minute "tiny victories" circle. "What's one thing your body or brain did this week that you're proud of?" Her daughter draws a leaf labeled, "I asked for help in math." Her son writes, "Didn't punch the wall when I was mad." Maya writes, "I pulled over instead of pushing through."

The tree on the wall grows by three small leaves. So does her sense that healing, in this house, is becoming routine.

By Sunday, Maya still feels tired. Healing has not made her life easy. But there is a different tone in the home. Bedtime includes a short body scan with her son—"Where is your Guard tonight?"—and a ritual with her daughter of choosing one hope for the week ahead. Maya keeps a BWI reflection sheet in her journal, not as a grading system, but as a way to notice patterns: sleep slightly better, anger a little less explosive, more moments of laughter returning. She is still living in a city shaped by inequity and stress. Yet inside this small household, practice has become a quiet form of resistance: tiny, repeated acts that teach three nervous systems that rest, boundary, and connection are allowed here.

## A Community Health Worker's Week When Healing Becomes Practice

Jordan's calendar looks like a tangle of color blocks: home visits, school meetings, Resilience Studio™ hours, case conferences, text check-ins with youth, and a weekly staff grounding circle. On paper, it could be another recipe for burnout. But since the team began using the Brain Well-Being Model® and Collective Care in Action® tools, Jordan's week has changed in small but important ways.

On Monday, before the Resilience Studio™ opens, Jordan walks the space slowly. They dim the overhead lights, straighten art supplies, and place Seeds cards at the entrance table. Then, as part of the team's new opening ritual, they and two colleagues stand near the ARTGard wall for a three-minute check-in. Each person names their current mode (Guard, Healing, or Thrive), one sensation in their body, and one boundary for the day. "I'm Guard and buzzy," Jordan says. "My boundary is no new intakes after 3 p.m." A year ago, naming such limits would have felt like failure. Now it is understood as nervous system maintenance. Their supervisor nods and adjusts the schedule accordingly.

On Wednesday, Jordan spends the morning supporting a small group of middle schoolers in the studio. The group begins with ten minutes of unstructured play and art: clay, markers, and quiet music in the background. This is not extra time. It is the somatic portion of the Brain Well-Being sequence. As the group settles, Jordan invites them into a quick Seeds reflection. "Draw how your body felt walking into school today." When one student draws a stick figure with a storm cloud over its head, Jordan gently asks, "Is that more Guard or more Healing?" The youth rolls their eyes but eventually shrugs. "Guard. I thought there was going to be a fight." The group spends a few minutes mapping where Guard shows up in their school day, using the language they have learned over months. It is messy, sometimes silly, sometimes sharp. But it is practice. Perceptual awareness is growing in context.

Later that day, Jordan sits in on a care coordination meeting with a school counselor, a teacher, and a caregiver. Instead of reporting only anecdotes, Jordan brings a simple Brain Well-Being Index summary for the youth they have been seeing. Somatic scores are inching upward, relational scores are improving slightly, and aspirational items remain low. "They're starting to use the art table and ask for breaks instead of walking out," Jordan explains. "But they still can't picture themselves here next year." The team uses this information as a map rather than a judgment. Together they create one small aspirational step: helping the student apply to a summer art program. Jordan leaves the meeting with a sense that data and story are finally working together.

By Friday, Jordan's own nervous system is showing signs of strain: a tight jaw, headaches, and growing irritability. In the past, they might have pushed through until collapsing on Saturday. Instead, they use the F.L.O.W.S. framework during their lunch break, jotting notes in a small notebook. They begin by naming what they feel: tension and fatigue. They locate the sensations in their shoulders and temples. They open space with three slow breaths and step outside briefly into sunlight. They witness the story forming in their mind: "I have to be everything for everyone." Then they shift one small thing they can control. They ask a colleague to co-facilitate the late afternoon group and block thirty minutes for quiet documentation time. None of these steps remove the structural pressures they face, but they prevent Jordan from abandoning their own body in the name of service.

On Saturday, Jordan joins a community gardening day at an ARTGard site affiliated with the Resilience Studio™. This is technically programming, but it also functions as restoration for families and for staff. Children dig and plant while elders sit under shade tents sharing stories. A local musician plays as volunteers water new seedlings. As Jordan moves between garden beds answering questions about soil and snails, they notice their own breath slowing. This, too, is Collective Care in Action®: a place where somatic, relational, and aspirational awareness weave together without anyone needing to name them directly.

By the end of the week, Jordan is still tired. The community's structural realities have not changed overnight. But instead of feeling like a lone, overfunctioning hero, Jordan feels part of a small ecosystem of practice: colleagues who normalize naming Guard, leadership that protects boundaries, youth who are learning to map their own nervous system states, and a neighborhood beginning to recognize the Resilience Studio™ and ARTGard as shared resources. Healing, in Jordan's world, is no longer an abstract goal. It is embedded in how meetings begin, how days end, how data are interpreted, and how people care for their own bodies in the middle of everyone else's storms.

## Layers of Practice: From Self to Community

When healing becomes practice, it moves through layers. It begins in individual bodies, is reinforced in families, is protected in teams and workplaces, and is amplified in communities. The same tools—Seeds and Leaves, the Brain Well-Being Index™, the F.L.O.W.S. framework, and ARTGard—can function differently at each layer while still serving the same purpose: helping nervous systems move from Guard toward Healing and Thrive.

### 1. Individual Practice: Returning to Your Own Body

At the individual layer, practice is about learning to recognize and respond to your own Guard patterns with compassion rather than criticism.

Examples of individual practice include:

● **Somatic check-ins**

Two-minute body scans in the morning or before challenging tasks: feet on the floor, notice the breath, name the current mode (Guard, Healing, Thrive), and adjust one small thing such as posture, breath, or pace.

**• F.L.O.W.S. self-reflection**

Using the F.L.O.W.S. sequence when activated, Feel, Locate, Open, Witness, Shift, to create a small pause before reacting.

**• BWI personal snapshots**

Completing a brief Brain Well-Being Index reflection once a week or once a month, not as a scorecard but as a way to notice patterns in somatic, perceptual, relational, and aspirational awareness.

These practices do not remove structural stress, but they protect one critical relationship: the one between you and your own nervous system.

---

## 2. Family and Household Practice: Changing the Tone of Home

At the family layer, practice focuses on making regulation, reflection, and connection part of the rhythm of the household.

Examples of family practice include:

**• Seeds at arrival, Leaves at closing**

Using Seeds cards for short check-ins, "How are you arriving?" and Leaves cards for tiny victories or shifts, "What changed even a little today?" Over time, families can build a visible tree that reflects these moments of growth.

- **Guard and Healing language in daily conversation**

Normalizing phrases such as "My body is in Guard right now" or "What would help us move toward Healing?" rather than labeling people as "good" or "bad."

- **Micro-rituals of rest and play**

Short, predictable moments such as a song before bed, a five-minute dance break after homework, or a weekly walk without screens. These practices teach the body that joy and rest are allowed rather than something that must be earned.

In these homes, practice does not mean perfection. It means that nervous systems have more places to land.

**3. Team and Workplace Practice: Protecting Helpers**

For teams, agencies, schools, and Resilience Studios™, practice means building cultures where staff and volunteers are not sacrificed in the name of service.

Examples of team practice include:

- **Mode and body check-ins**: Opening staff meetings or shifts with a brief round where each person names their mode (Guard, Healing, Thrive), one body sensation, and one boundary for the day. When entire teams are in Guard, workloads can be adjusted accordingly.

- **F.L.O.W.S. for debrief and supervision**: Using the F.L.O.W.S. framework in supervision or case review to attend to what each person felt and carried in their body, not only to tasks and outcomes.

- **BWI-informed team reflection**: Looking at aggregate BWI patterns from staff and participants to ask environmental questions. What about our environment is keeping us in Guard? What changes in schedule, space, or policy might support movement toward Healing?

These practices recognize that staff nervous systems are part of the intervention, not invisible background conditions.

## 4. Community Practice: Making Collective Care Visible

At the community layer, practice involves shared rituals, spaces, and agreements that make regulation and belonging more likely for everyone.

Examples of community practice include:

- **Community play and ARTGard days**: Regular gatherings where children, youth, and adults engage in art, gardening, music, and movement together. These spaces support somatic and relational awareness without requiring clinical language.

- **Shared language in public spaces**: Churches, schools, barbershops, and youth programs incorporating Guard, Healing, and Thrive language into flyers, sermons, classroom norms, and group agreements so that nervous system literacy becomes part of everyday culture.

- **Collective reflection moments**: Neighborhood meetings, parent circles, or youth councils opening with Seeds-style check-ins and closing with Leaves-style reflections or hopes. In this way, Brain Well-Being practices become woven into civic life.

Across these layers, practice is not about doing everything at once. It is about choosing a few simple, repeatable actions that align with the Brain Well-Being Model® and allowing them to accumulate over time.

## F.L.O.W.S.: A Simple Framework for Everyday Moments

F.L.O.W.S. began as a staff reflection tool in Resilience Studios™ and wellness labs. It quickly became clear that it was useful far beyond debrief meetings. It offers a simple, repeatable sequence that helps the nervous system move from pure reaction toward a little more space and choice—whether you are a caregiver in a car, a youth in a classroom, or a CHW leaving a home visit.

F.L.O.W.S. stands for:

- Feel: Notice what is happening in your body right now. Heat in your face, tightness in your jaw, buzzing muscles, heaviness in your chest, numbness. No fixing yet—just sensing.

- Locate: Name where in your body the experience lives most strongly. "It's in my stomach," "It's in my shoulders," "My throat feels tight." Locating turns a vague storm into something more specific and manageable.

- Open: Create a little more room around the sensation. This might be three slower breaths, unclenching your hands, loosening your jaw, shifting your posture, or stepping outside for a moment. Opening does not mean erasing. It means making enough space that Guard is not driving everything.

- Witness: Notice the story your mind is telling about what is happening. "They don't respect me." "I always mess this up." "We are not safe here." Witnessing does not argue with the story; it simply recognizes, This is the narrative my Guard Mode is offering right now.

- Shift: Choose one small, doable action that supports Healing or Thrive. This might be asking for a pause, sending a text for backup, drinking water, changing the order of tasks, or returning to the conversation later. The shift is not the whole solution. It is the next kind step.

F.L.O.W.S. does not change housing policy or undo historical trauma. It does something more modest and equally essential: it gives people a way to stay in relationship with their own nervous system and with one another in the middle of stress. When practiced regularly, individually and in teams, it becomes a shared culture of pausing, noticing, and choosing together.

**Everyday Tools: Seeds, Leaves, and BWI Reflection**

Alongside F.L.O.W.S., three everyday tools, Seeds, Leaves, and simple BWI reflections, carry much of the daily work of practice in homes, studios, schools, and community spaces.

**Seeds: Naming How We Arrive**

Seeds cards invite a quick picture or word that answers a simple question: how am I arriving in this moment or space? They are most powerful when used without pressure or over explanation.

- **In families**, Seeds can live on a kitchen table or refrigerator, used at breakfast or bedtime as a way to check in without forcing long conversations.

- **In Resilience Studios™ and classrooms**, Seeds at the door help adults notice patterns. Over time they begin to see who often arrives in Guard, whose mode shifts across the week, and when collective Guard rises across a group.

- **For individuals**, a single Seed drawn in a journal at the start of the day can become a quiet act of self honesty.

Seeds primarily support somatic and perceptual awareness. They help people notice how their bodies and stories are walking into the room.

## Leaves: Noticing What Has Shifted

Leaves cards ask a different question: what, if anything, feels even a little different after being here? Sometimes the change is noticeable and significant. Often it is small. Occasionally the answer is simply "no change," which is equally welcome.

- **Families** may use Leaves at the end of the day or week to name tiny victories such as "I asked for help," "I rested," "I did not yell," or "Nothing changed and I showed up anyway."

- **Studios, youth groups, and classrooms** may add Leaves to a shared tree or wall so that change becomes visible over time, even when daily life still feels difficult.

- **Providers and community health workers** often use Leaves reflections to remind themselves that small shifts in sleep, connection, or hope matter, especially when larger systems move slowly.

Leaves sit mainly in the relational and aspirational domains. They record connection, meaning, and possibility in small, concrete ways.

## BWI Reflection: Seeing Patterns Over Time

The full Brain Well Being Index is designed for structured use in clinical, educational, and community settings. Its four domains, somatic, perceptual, relational, and aspirational, also lend themselves to informal reflection practices.

- **Individuals and caregivers** can complete short BWI reflection sheets monthly as a way to notice patterns. Is the body slightly less in Guard? Are personal stories softening? Is there a little more connection or hope than three months ago?

- **Teams** can review aggregated patterns and ask environmental questions. Why are somatic scores consistently low in this program? What about the schedule, space, or expectations might be keeping bodies in Guard?

- **Community partners** may use BWI snapshots before and after a season of programming or a new initiative. The goal is to ask not only "Did people like it?" but also "Did it support movement toward Healing and Thrive?"

In all of these settings, BWI reflection is not about perfection or performance. It is about witnessing movement that may be slow, uneven, and gradual so that people do not have to rely on memory alone to believe that change is happening.

Together, F.L.O.W.S., Seeds, Leaves, and BWI reflection offer a simple toolkit for making healing a daily practice rather than an occasional event. The next chapter turns from tools to time, exploring how these practices, repeated across seasons and generations, begin to shape the world we needed and the one our children deserve.

# Chapter 15

# Beginning the World We Needed

After school, my son drops into the passenger seat, backpack on the floor and phone already in his hand. I ask how it was, mostly talking to the side of his hoodie, and he answers with one word: "Fine." His eyes stay on the screen, one shoulder a little higher than usual, and I feel my own Guard rise. Old stories about respect surface, along with fear for his safety in a world that does not always hold Black boys gently. I feel the urge to lecture or to pull more out of him than he has to give today. Instead, I put both feet on the floor, feel my hands on the steering wheel, and take one quiet breath he will never notice.

"You want sushi," I ask, "or you just want me to drive?"

"Sushi." No hesitation. That is the real question between us most days anyway.

We pull off toward our spot, the little place that knows our faces and our usual order. He taps his phone while we wait, hood still up, offering a few thin sentences about teachers, friends, and drama I only half understand. I do not turn it into a lesson about phones, gratitude, or how lucky he is to have this. I let the ritual be what it is: soy sauce, shared rolls, familiar chairs, and his shoulders slowly dropping as he eats. I am not getting a perfect, poster ready moment of emotional disclosure. I am getting something quieter. It is proof that my body is doing something different from what raised me. I am meeting his Guard with more softness and steadiness than the world ever met mine.

This is where "the world we needed" begins for me. It does not begin in a policy brief or a program proposal. It begins in the way I choose to sit with my thirteen year old, order sushi, breathe, and refuse to make him earn my calm. Parenting, in this moment, becomes one of the places where Collective Care in Action® stops being theory and becomes dinner.

Every generation inherits a world it did not design. Some inherit stability. Some inherit uncertainty. Some inherit wounds that were never named, systems that were never just, and histories still living inside the body. This generation has inherited a nervous system shaped by chronic stress and, at the same time, an unprecedented understanding of how healing actually happens. The question before us is no longer only clinical. It is civilizational: What kind of world do we choose to build with what we now know?

## Healing Was Never Rare, Only Unsupported

Across cultures and centuries, communities have always practiced forms of regulation and care. Songs shared in grief, hands placed gently on a shoulder, stories told to create meaning, rhythms repeated until breathing slows, gardens grown in difficult soil, meals prepared when words are not enough, children allowed to play even in the shadow of uncertainty, and love carried quietly across generations. None of this is new.

What has been missing is not wisdom, but permission, structure, and shared belief strong enough to protect these practices inside modern systems. This book does not introduce healing to the world. It restores legitimacy to what communities have known all along.

## From Individual Relief to Collective Design

For decades, mental health has focused, necessarily, on helping individuals survive distress through therapy rooms, crisis lines, clinical treatment, diagnosis, and stabilization. All of this is essential. All of it saves lives. But survival alone cannot be the final horizon of human possibility.

When distress is shaped by the environment, healing must also reshape the environment. When trauma is collective, care must become collective. When regulation is relational, systems must become relational as well.

This is the turning point: healing moving from private relief toward public design.

## The Future of Care Is Collective

Collective Care in Action® is not a single program, intervention, or institution. It represents a shift in worldview. We do not heal alone. We do not thrive in isolation. We do not regulate without a relationship.

No system can produce well-being while ignoring the environments where people actually live.

Collective care therefore asks different questions. Do children feel safe enough to learn? Do families have enough stability to rest? Do communities have spaces for joy, culture, and play? Do helpers receive the support required to keep helping? Do policies reduce stress, or quietly multiply it?

Wherever the answers begin to move toward safety, thriving becomes biologically possible.

## From Guard Mode to Thrive Mode at Scale

Imagine environments intentionally designed to support nervous system well-being. Classrooms organized around regulation and belonging. Health systems measuring safety and connection. Community spaces resourced for creativity and play. Youth trusted as leaders in wellness. Caregivers supported before burnout begins. Culture honored as medicine rather than ornament. Prevention is valued as much as treatment.

This is not fantasy. Pieces of this future already exist in schools, clinics, churches, neighborhoods, and movements led by people who refused to believe survival was the best humanity could do. The task now is alignment.

## Evidence, Workforce, and Systems Together

Lasting transformation requires three movements converging at once.

**Evidence:** Research that confirms what communities experience. Safety, relationship, and environment shape mental health as powerfully as treatment.

**Workforce:** People prepared, trusted, and sustained to carry healing into daily life. This includes clinicians, community health workers, doulas, peer specialists, educators, faith leaders, artists, youth, and families themselves.

**Systems:** Policies and institutions willing to invest upstream in prevention, equity, belonging, and the biological conditions of thriving.

When these three move together, change accelerates from possibility to reality. That acceleration has already begun.

## Why Play Remains Central

At the center of this entire vision lives something disarmingly simple: play. Not as entertainment, reward, or distraction, but as biology.

Play signals safety. It restores flexibility. It invites connection and rehearses possibility. It tells the nervous system that life is more than survival.

When joy becomes normal again, futures change. The shift is not abstract. It is neurological, relational, and collective. Protecting play may be one of the most serious public health decisions a society can make.

## A Threshold Moment

There are moments in history when knowledge expands faster than systems, when old structures can no longer carry what humanity has learned. We are living inside one of those moments now.

We understand trauma more deeply than any generation before. We understand development, attachment, and regulation with unprecedented clarity. We understand the biological cost of inequity.

That means something new is possible. We can choose differently, on purpose.

## The Invitation

I do not practice any of this perfectly. My son would probably describe our evenings in terms of sushi orders and side-eye, not "intergenerational healing." But every time I choose breath over explosion, curiosity over control, or a quiet meal over another lecture, I am beginning a different world for him and for the thirteen-year-old I once was.

You are not asked to solve everything or transform systems alone. You are not expected to carry more than is human to carry.

The invitation is simpler and more powerful: notice where healing is already trying to happen, protect moments of safety, practice connection when possible, create small spaces where joy can return, support the people doing this work, and design environments that make these choices easier for the next person and the next generation.

This is how worlds change. Rarely all at once. Almost always through ordinary courage repeated.

Healing is not the absence of harm. It is the presence of connection, play, safety, love, dignity, belonging, and possibility lived out in ordinary days.

We were never meant to heal alone.

Beginning now, with breath, with relationship, with practice, and with design, we do not have to.

# Chapter 16

# Culturally Intelligent Care in Systems Practice

By the time healing reaches the level of systems, a deeper question emerges: What does it mean for care itself to become trustworthy?

For many communities shaped by historical exclusion, medical harm, and structural inequity, distress is not only personal. It is relational, institutional, and intergenerational. When harm has been systemic, healing cannot rely on clinical skill alone. It must include cultural intelligence. Cultural intelligence is the capacity of systems to recognize how history lives in bodies and to organize care in ways that communicate safety rather than threat.

For decades, health and mental health systems have pursued cultural competence, the effort to understand and respectfully serve diverse populations. That work mattered. It opened doors, named inequities, and challenged silence. Yet competence alone is not enough for communities whose nervous systems have learned caution through lived experience. Cultural competence can still center the institution's perspective: what it knows, what it offers, and how it believes it is performing. Cultural intelligence moves further. It asks not only whether a system understands a community, but whether that community has experienced the system as safe. Safety is not declared by institutions. It is felt by people.

This shift reflects a broader movement in relational science, from individual therapeutic attunement to system-wide regulatory design. More than a century ago, psychoanalyst Sándor Ferenczi challenged the emotional distance that dominated early therapeutic practice. He argued that trauma required not neutrality, but attuned responsiveness and relational flexibility. Ferenczi insisted that empathy itself was therapeutic and that early relational injury must be taken seriously. Decades later, attachment research and polyvagal-informed neuroscience provided biological explanations for what he intuited: nervous systems shift toward regulation not through interpretation alone, but through felt safety.

Within systems practice, radical empathy is not sentimentality. It is structural. It requires institutions to examine how tone, pacing, humility, flexibility, and repair function as biological signals. When communities have experienced harm through systems, repair begins not with efficiency but with attuned presence. Empathy, practiced within ethical boundaries, becomes a regulatory intervention. It communicates that invisibility is ending.

Institutions regulate human bodies whether intentionally or not. Policies signal safety or threat. Waiting rooms signal dignity or dismissal. Provider tone signals partnership or hierarchy. Access barriers signal welcome or exclusion. Attachment science demonstrates that human beings organize expectations of safety through consistent relational experience. Polyvagal-informed neuroscience clarifies that the autonomic nervous system continuously scans social environments for cues of safety or danger. These principles extend beyond therapy rooms. A school discipline policy can function as a cue of safety or a cue of threat. A benefits application process can reduce vigilance or reinforce it.

In one neighborhood clinic, this shift began with a simple question from community health workers: "What does this place feel like in your body when you walk in?" People described stiffness in their shoulders, tight jaws, and memories of being dismissed or rushed. The intake process happened behind glass. Forms came before eye contact. No one explained what would happen next. The clinic was delivering services, but patients' nervous systems were reading the setting as a place of threat rather than care.

Together, CHWs, front desk staff, clinicians, and community members redesigned the first five minutes of every visit. The glass barrier was removed. Chairs were rearranged so people could sit side by side. Intake staff were trained to begin with a warm greeting and a plain language explanation of what would happen that day before any paperwork. CHWs from the neighborhood met patients in the lobby, used familiar language and dress, and stayed in touch between visits by phone or text. Over time, more people kept follow-up appointments and began to describe the clinic as "somewhere I'm seen" instead of "a place I go when I'm in trouble." The medical services did not change as much as the cues of safety around them, and those cues were carried most powerfully by CHWs who already belonged to the community.

From a nervous system perspective, systems themselves participate in regulation. Cultural intelligence is therefore not an added program. It is a redesign of relational experience inside institutions.

Structured relational models such as Theraplay and the Attachment, Regulation, and Competency framework translate attachment science into practical strategies of predictability, attunement, co-regulation, emotional literacy, and repair. Although developed to support children and families affected by trauma, their principles extend naturally into organizational life. Predictability reduces hypervigilance. Attunement reduces defensive arousal. Repair restores trust. Shared power strengthens belonging. These are not simply therapeutic techniques. They are blueprints for institutional behavior.

The Compassionate Systems of Awareness framework further extends relational and nervous system science into schools and organizations. Rather than treating trauma as an individual condition, it examines how entire systems influence collective regulation. Leadership, meeting structures, communication patterns, and disciplinary practices are recognized as contributors to either collective stress or collective resilience. Compassion is reframed not as personality, but as infrastructure. It becomes something that can be designed, practiced, and measured.

The Brain Well-Being Model® organizes these traditions into four observable domains of awareness: somatic, perceptual, relational, and aspirational. These domains make safety measurable and teachable across healthcare, schools, and community settings. Collective Care in Action® translates this shared language into workforce and systems infrastructure. When staff, leaders, and partners are thinking within the same four domains, regulation stops being mysterious and becomes something a team can intentionally design.

Sustainable systems require preparation across diverse community-based healing roles. Community health workers, peer support specialists, doulas, youth leaders, wellness coaches, educators, faith partners, and community-based organizations form the relational network through which regulation becomes continuous rather than episodic. Shared language reduces fragmentation. When providers, school staff, managed care partners, and community members can recognize Guard Mode, Healing Mode, and Thrive Mode across settings, coordination becomes biologically coherent rather than administratively siloed.

Culturally intelligent systems consistently share several characteristics. Historical truth is acknowledged and communities are not asked to forget what harmed them. Community knowledge is treated as expertise, and lived experience stands beside clinical training. Access is simplified. Relationships are continuous. Joy and culture are visible within care environments. These are not symbolic gestures. Each functions as a cue of safety that influences autonomic regulation, reduces defensive arousal, and increases capacity for trust and collaboration.

Within Collective Care in Action®, these elements are observed and tracked rather than assumed. The Brain Well-Being Index provides a reflective framework for identifying shifts in regulation, relational trust, and aspirational capacity across individuals and systems over time. Instead of asking only, "Did we deliver services?" systems can begin asking, "Did bodies feel safer here? Did people experience more connection and possibility after engaging with us?"

Culturally intelligent care cannot exist without a workforce intentionally prepared to function as regulatory infrastructure.

These roles create continuity across environments. Through shared language, relational presence, and cultural fluency, they transmit cues of safety that no policy alone can deliver. When workforce becomes infrastructure, collective healing becomes sustainable.

Fragmented systems often fail not because of a lack of effort, but because of a lack of shared understanding. When educators, clinicians, community health workers, and community members use different frameworks to describe distress, coordination weakens. The Brain Well-Being Model® offers a common vocabulary that transcends professional silos. Shared language reduces misinterpretation, increases collaboration, and supports prevention rather than crisis response. Regulation becomes a community competency rather than a specialized intervention.

Across healthcare reform, school wellness investments, workforce expansion initiatives, and public health transformation efforts, systems are already moving toward integrated and prevention-oriented models. What remains uneven is the language and structure for embedding regulation science into that movement. The Brain Well-Being Model® and Collective Care in Action® do not introduce a new direction. They organize what evidence and community practice are already revealing: safety, belonging, and relational continuity are infrastructure.

In California, the CalAIM initiative offers one example of this shift. By adding community health workers and doulas as Medi-Cal benefits through Enhanced Care Management and Community Supports, the state has begun treating trusted, culturally rooted helpers as core infrastructure rather than extras. Managed care plans are being asked to coordinate physical, behavioral, and social supports, bring care into communities rather than only into clinics, and focus attention on members with the highest levels of need and inequity. At its best, this shift moves systems closer to what communities have asked for all along: whole-person, prevention-oriented care delivered by people and organizations that feel familiar, trustworthy, and capable of walking with families over time.

In many ways, CalAIM represents one state's attempt to address a problem that exists nationwide and even globally: the lack of connectivity between the places where people live, the systems that pay for care, and the relationships that actually help them heal. By funding Community Supports and community health workers, CalAIM begins to treat connection itself as infrastructure. Clinics are linked to housing supports. Behavioral health services are connected to community programs. Health plans partner with neighborhood organizations. Other states and countries are watching closely, not to copy California's exact structure, but to learn how a large public system can invest in relationships, navigation, and social supports as seriously as it invests in procedures.

This is the heart of Collective Care in Action®: turning what has often been an invisible network of care into an intentional, resourced, and coordinated ecosystem.

The future of equitable care will not be defined by whether harm ever occurred. Harm is part of human history. The future will be defined by whether systems can repair. Repair requires listening without defensiveness, changing without delay, sharing power, and remaining present long enough for trust to return.

When systems recognize that regulation is relational, that culture is regulatory, and that workforce is infrastructure, care reorganizes itself around prevention and belonging. The future of healing will not be built by isolated expertise. It will be built by coordinated courage. And that courage begins wherever leaders decide that safety is not incidental to care, but foundational to it.

# Chapter 17

# From Guard Mode to Collective Thriving

Every generation inherits conditions it did not choose. Some inherit stability. Others inherit survival. This generation has inherited something historically unusual: a world where chronic stress has become normalized across entire populations. Rising anxiety, widening inequities, community violence, isolation, burnout, and disconnection are individually painful and collectively dangerous. When Guard Mode becomes widespread, societies begin organizing around protection instead of possibility.

## The Limits of Individual Healing

For decades, mental health has focused primarily on the individual: therapy sessions, diagnoses, treatment plans, and coping skills. All of these are essential. All of them save lives. Yet they remain incomplete on their own.

Many drivers of distress are structural rather than personal. Housing instability, economic pressure, racism, educational inequity, community violence, and barriers to health care access shape nervous system experience long before an individual ever enters a therapy room. No individual intervention, no matter how excellent, can fully resolve collective conditions.

The question therefore evolves. It is no longer only, "How do we help people heal?" It becomes, "How do we help communities regulate?"

**Collective Regulation as Public Health**

Neuroscience now confirms what many cultures have always practiced: humans regulate together. Safety spreads through relationship. Calm spreads through environment. Hope spreads through the visible presence of possibility. Collective thriving is not simply a metaphor. It is a biological reality.

When communities gain stable housing, safe schools, accessible care, trusted relationships, cultural belonging, and economic opportunity, nervous systems shift not one by one, but together. Fewer bodies live in constant Guard Mode. More people are able to move into Healing Mode and, at times, Thrive Mode. Public health, at its deepest level, becomes nervous system regulation at scale.

This is why collective care cannot be treated as an extra in policy and planning. It is the connective tissue that allows prevention, treatment, and recovery to actually reach people's lives rather than remaining isolated programs.

## Evidence That Thriving Is Possible

Across the world, signals of transformation are already emerging. Trauma-informed school systems are improving behavior and learning by prioritizing regulation over punishment. Community health worker and promotor(a) models are increasing access and trust by meeting people where they are. Birth equity initiatives are reducing maternal risk by centering the safety and voices of Black and Brown parents. Arts in health programs are supporting emotional regulation.

Nature-based interventions are lowering stress physiology. Peer support is reducing hospitalization and isolation.

These are not isolated innovations. They represent early architecture for a different future, one in which thriving is not rare but expected. They show that when environments change, patterns in bodies and communities change with them.

## Designing for the Next Generation

Children growing up today will inherit whatever systems we build now. If systems remain organized around crisis, they will inherit survival. If systems reorganize around safety, they will inherit possibility. The work of collective thriving is therefore not abstract. It is an intergenerational responsibility.

Designing for collective thriving means asking, at every level, what a policy, practice, or space teaches a child's nervous system to expect from the world. Does it teach that asking for help is dangerous or welcome? Does it teach that mistakes lead to humiliation or to repair? Does it teach that culture is something to hide or something that belongs at the center of life? When we design with these questions in mind, we are not only changing services. We are changing what "normal" feels like in a body.

This work requires courage in the present. It requires the courage to design environments our ancestors were denied but our children deserve.

### From Guarded Systems to Collective Thriving

Guard Mode is not only an individual state. It can become a system's default condition. Institutions that have been under-resourced, overburdened, or shaped by punitive histories often begin to behave like guarded bodies. Policies become rigid. Communication becomes defensive. Flexibility decreases. Threat responses accelerate. Creativity and repair become rare.

In this sense, many of our current structures are themselves operating in Guard Mode.

Collective thriving asks systems to move through their own version of healing: telling the truth about harm, slowing down enough to listen, sharing power, and investing in prevention instead of clinging to crisis. When schools, clinics, health plans, and community agencies begin to function less like isolated, guarded units and more like parts of a shared ecosystem, new possibilities emerge. Data can be used to understand patterns rather than to punish. Funding can support relationships and continuity rather than focusing only on procedures. Workforce can be treated as regulatory infrastructure rather than expendable labor.

In California, initiatives such as CalAIM illustrate both the promise and the challenge of this shift. By recognizing community health workers, doulas, and community supports as reimbursable care, the state is attempting to value connection, navigation, and housing stability as seriously as it values medical procedures. At their best, these efforts move systems toward what communities have asked for all along: whole person care delivered by trusted people in familiar places. At their worst, they risk becoming another layer of complexity if they are not grounded in shared language, cultural intelligence, and genuine partnership with communities. The difference between those outcomes is not only policy. It depends on whether collective care truly becomes the organizing logic.

# The Threshold of Change

Human history rarely shifts gradually. It shifts when understanding becomes impossible to ignore. We now understand that trauma is biological, that healing is relational, that environment shapes mental health, that equity shapes life expectancy, that connection protects survival, and that joy supports resilience. Most importantly, we understand that thriving can be intentionally designed.

Standing at this threshold, the remaining question is no longer scientific. It is moral and practical: Will we build the world we now know is possible? Will we organize systems around the biology of safety and belonging, or continue asking individuals to heal inside structures that repeatedly pull them back into Guard Mode?

This is also an intergenerational question. The choices we make now about policy, funding, workforce, and culture will shape what "normal" feels like in the bodies of children who have not yet learned the word trauma. We can continue passing down nervous systems organized around vigilance and overfunctioning, or we can begin passing down nervous systems that recognize rest, play, and connection as part of everyday life.

The final chapter turns toward the most disarming part of that redesign: play. If collective thriving is the destination, then play is one of the clearest signals that we are moving in the right direction. The question that remains is both simple and profound: What happens when we take play seriously enough to design for it now, so that the next generation can thrive later?

Chapter 18

# Play Now. Thrive Later.

If collective thriving is the destination, play is one of the clearest signals that we are moving in the right direction. Wherever real play returns, nervous systems quietly learn that life can be more than survival. Every meaningful movement begins with a shift in imagination, a moment when people begin to believe that the future does not have to repeat the past. This book was written inside such a moment.

## Why Play Matters More Than We Were Taught

Play is often misunderstood as leisure: optional, childlike, and unnecessary in serious times. Biology tells a different story. Play regulates the nervous system, strengthens relationships, expands creativity, supports learning, builds resilience, and restores hope. Across species, play appears wherever survival is no longer the only priority. That leads to something quietly radical. Play is evidence of safety.

When children, youth, or adults are able to play, their bodies receive a message very different from the one carried by Guard Mode. Play tells the nervous system that it can loosen its grip, even if only a little. It signals that a person is safe enough to explore, laugh, and try again. In environments shaped by chronic stress, that message is not trivial. It is corrective. It begins to rewrite the expectation that life is only about bracing for impact.

Wherever play returns, whether in classrooms, Resilience Studios™, ARTGard spaces, living rooms, faith communities, parks, or digital environments designed with care, thriving can begin. This process rarely happens all at once and rarely follows a perfect or linear path. Instead, it unfolds through small moments in which joy and curiosity return to places that once held only vigilance and fatigue.

## The Philosophy of *"Play Now. Thrive Later."*

The phrase is simple, but its implications are profound. "Play Now. Thrive Later." suggests that thriving is not created later through achievement alone. It is built now through experiences that teach the nervous system three essential truths:

- You are safe enough to explore.

- You are connected enough to belong.

- You are supported enough to imagine a future.

When children receive these conditions early, their brains organize around possibility instead of protection. The architecture of their nervous systems changes. Stress responses still exist, but they no longer dominate the system. Instead, they become one pathway among many.

When communities receive these conditions collectively, not only in a single program or classroom but across schools, clinics, streets, screens, and homes, history begins to shift direction. The patterns carried across generations can begin to reorganize.

Play now, in this sense, is not a distraction from real work. It is real work at the level of biology and culture. A school that protects recess and arts as fiercely as test preparation sends children a message about their worth that no slogan can replace. A clinic that includes play in waiting rooms, groups, and Resilience Studios™ tells families that their joy matters, not only their symptoms. A city that invests in safe parks, gardens, and youth programs is investing in the long-term health of its own nervous system.

*"Play Now. Thrive Later."* is also a promise to our younger selves. Many people did not grow up with the safety needed to play freely. They learned instead to be careful, helpful, invisible, or hypervigilant. Creating playful and regulated spaces today is one way to offer the next generation what many adults once needed. In the process, it also allows our own bodies to experience a different kind of normal.

## A Call Beyond the Page

Books do not transform the world on their own. People do. For that reason, the final invitation of this work is not primarily intellectual. It is practical.

- Create one safer space.

- Protect one moment of play.

- Strengthen one relationship.

- Reduce one barrier to care.

- Support one child's curiosity.

- Invest in one community's well-being.

These actions rarely look dramatic. They might appear as a teacher pausing to play a five-minute game before a difficult lesson. They might look like a caregiver choosing to sit on the floor and draw for a few minutes instead of offering another lecture. They might take the form of a supervisor protecting time for staff joy in the middle of a heavy caseload. They might be a plan partner choosing to fund a neighborhood ARTGard or Resilience Studio™ instead of investing only in clinic visits.

Small actions, repeated collectively, become systems change. When many people in many roles make choices like these, the texture of everyday life begins to shift. Guard Mode loosens its grip. Healing becomes more accessible. Thrive Mode moves from theory into lived practice.

## The Future Within Reach

Imagine a generation raised where:

- Mental health is taught alongside literacy, not only after a crisis.

- Play is protected as prevention, not treated as a reward.

- Care is culturally intelligent, not just technically competent.

- Communities are resourced with dignity, not only with emergency relief.

- Healing is collective, not isolated.

- Thriving is normal, not rare.

This is not fantasy. It is alignment—of science, compassion, and courage. Alignment happens when our policies, budgets, schedules, supervision practices, curricula, and design choices all begin to point in the same direction: toward safety, belonging, and possibility.

In earlier chapters, we named evidence, workforce, and systems as three strands that must move together. *"Play Now. Thrive Later."* weaves through all three. Evidence shows that play supports regulation and resilience. Workforce, community health workers, educators, clinicians, artists, caregivers, youth leaders, becomes the living conduit through which play is invited and protected. Systems decide whether there will be time, space, and resources for any of it to exist beyond the margins.

Alignment is how history moves. When enough people, in enough places, refuse to treat joy as disposable, the future shifts.

## The Final Truth Beneath Everything

Across every chapter, one idea keeps returning: humans were never meant to survive alone, and they have always been capable of thriving together. If this book has offered language, direction, or hope, even in the smallest way, then its purpose is already unfolding. The real work was never meant to end here.

It continues wherever someone chooses connection over isolation, curiosity over fear, care over indifference, play over despair, and possibility over resignation. These choices rarely make headlines. They do not always come with funding or fanfare. Yet they accumulate. In homes, classrooms, clinics, parks, studios, gardens, and digital spaces, they form the lived curriculum of a different world.

Through these choices, repeated across lives and communities, the future quietly begins to change.

# Where Healing Continues

Long after a book is finished, life keeps moving. Children still wake carrying invisible stories in their bodies. Families still search for language to name what they feel. Communities continue holding unbearable grief and unimaginable resilience at the same time. Nothing in these pages suggests that pain disappears easily or that history loosens its grip overnight.

And yet something else is also true. In quiet places rarely captured by headlines, healing is already happening. It happens when a caregiver pauses long enough for a child's nervous system to settle. It appears when neighbors gather without needing a formal reason. It grows when music fills a room that once held only silence, when hands touch soil and remember patience, and when laughter returns to a body that had forgotten it could.

These moments do not announce themselves as breakthroughs. They rarely look dramatic. Yet inside the nervous system they are profound. Every experience of genuine safety, no matter how small, teaches the brain a new possibility: survival is not the only future.

## The Work That Cannot End With a Book

If the ideas in this book matter, it is not because they are written here. It is because they can be practiced in places where no one is reading. Healing unfolds in classrooms before lessons begin, in clinics between appointments, and in kitchens after long days. It appears in churches, parks, barbershops, gardens, and living rooms where ordinary life continues.

Healing has never belonged to professionals alone. It has always lived in relationship. What changes now is not the existence of healing, but our willingness to recognize it, support it, and design systems that allow it to grow. When regulation, safety, and belonging are treated as shared responsibilities rather than private projects, collective care moves from idea to infrastructure.

## Carrying the Knowledge Forward

There will be moments when the world still feels unchanged. Systems may continue moving slowly. Inequities may still feel overwhelming. Guard Mode may appear again in bodies, families, and communities that have endured too much for too long. In those moments it may help to remember that transformation in human history rarely begins with certainty. It begins with people who choose to care differently before proof appears.

A regulated breath before a reaction.

A softer voice where harshness once lived.

A space created for play where none existed before.

A decision to remain connected when isolation would feel easier.

These actions are not small. They form the architecture of a different future being built in real time. They represent the kinds of choices that gradually reorganize what "normal" feels like, first for one person, then for a family, then for a neighborhood, and eventually for entire communities.

## What Healing Asks of Us

Healing does not require perfection or complete understanding. It does not wait for ideal conditions. Healing asks only that we notice where safety is possible, that we protect moments of connection, that we practice regulation together, and that we believe thriving is worthy of design rather than settling only for survival.

It asks us to continue choosing life giving relationships over protective isolation whenever we can. It asks us to protect play even when urgency attempts to erase it. It asks us to treat culture as medicine rather than decoration and to honor the wisdom of communities who practiced collective care long before models or acronyms existed to describe it.

## A Final Knowing

If you have reached this page, something has already shifted. Perhaps the change is not dramatic. Perhaps it cannot yet be explained easily in words. Yet somewhere in your body there may be a little more space to breathe, a little more curiosity than judgment, and a quiet sense that healing, once distant, might actually be possible.

If that is true, even in the smallest way, then the work of this book is already continuing beyond it. These ideas were never meant to remain inside pages. They were always meant to live in people.

## The Future Still Being Written

The world imagined here is not guaranteed. But it is possible, every place where children are met with gentleness, communities are resourced with dignity, culture is honored as medicine, play is protected as necessity, and connection is treated as essential infrastructure for life. This future will not arrive all at once. It will grow through ordinary moments repeated across many lives, quietly, collectively, persistently, the way healing always has.

## And So We Continue

Where this book ends, the real work begins. Not someday. Not somewhere else. Here, in the living spaces of daily life, carried forward by anyone willing to believe that safety can expand, that joy can return, and that communities can heal together. The deepest truth beneath every page remains simple: we were never meant to heal alone. The moment we begin to care for one another differently, the future begins to change.

# Brain Well-Being Index (BWI) Overview and Purpose

## How to Use This Appendix

This appendix is written for anyone who wants a simple way to understand and use the Brain Well-Being Index: clinicians, community health workers, educators, youth leaders, faith leaders, and families. You do not need a clinical license to make use of this tool. The following pages explain what the BWI measures, how it is structured, when to use it, and how to read scores as signs of movement in safety, connection, and hope rather than as labels. You can skim for what you need: a quick overview, the item list, guidance on timing, or ideas for how to bring BWI language into everyday conversations about healing.

## What the BWI Is

The Brain Well-Being Index (BWI) is a brief, non-diagnostic wellness and functioning index that complements traditional symptom screeners. It is designed to help providers, programs, and communities notice movement in somatic, perceptual, relational, and aspirational awareness over time, using simple items that can be completed in a few minutes.

Where tools like the PHQ-9 or GAD-7 focus on symptom severity, the BWI focuses on:

- regulation capacity

- functional stability

- engagement with life

- connection to hope and purpose

## Purpose

The BWI was created to:

- provide a simple, defensible way to track movement from Guard Mode toward Healing and Thrive Modes

- measure protective factors and recovery-oriented indicators, not just symptoms

- support measurement-based care in behavioral health, Enhanced Care Management (ECM), and community-based wellness services

- offer shared language that can be used across clinical, educational, and community settings

The BWI is not diagnostic and is not used for medical-necessity determinations or level-of-care decisions. Results are always interpreted within relational, cultural, and systemic context.

## Structure of the BWI

The BWI uses a 0–4 response scale:

- 0 = Not at all

- 1 = A little

- 2 = Sometimes

- 3 = Often

- 4 = Almost always

It includes 16 items grouped into four domains:

### Domain 1 – Somatic Awareness & Regulation

1. I am able to notice physical signs of stress in my body.

2. I have strategies that help me calm my body when I feel overwhelmed.

3. My sleep supports my daily functioning.

4. I feel physically regulated enough to manage daily responsibilities.

### Domain 2 – Perceptual Awareness

5. I can recognize how my thoughts affect my emotions and behaviors.

6. I am able to pause before reacting when something feels stressful.

7. I can identify when my stress response is increasing.

8.  I feel able to redirect unhelpful thought patterns when needed.

## Domain 3 – Relational Awareness

9.  I feel supported by at least one person or community.

10. I am able to communicate my needs to others.

11. My relationships feel mostly safe and manageable.

12. I know when to ask for help.

## Domain 4 – Aspirational Awareness

13. I feel connected to interests, goals, or activities that matter to me.

14. I have hope about my ability to move forward.

15. I feel motivated to engage in things that support my well-being.

16. I can imagine positive outcomes for myself or my family.

## Scoring and Interpretation

- Total score range: 0–64

- Domain scores: can be viewed independently or alongside the total score.

**In general:**

- Lower scores suggest reduced regulation and engagement (more time in Guard Mode states).

- Higher scores suggest increased stability, connection, and wellness (more access to Healing and Thrive Modes).

**Key principles:**

- Scores reflect state, not identity.

- Movement over time is more meaningful than any single score.

- Patterns across domains often matter more than the exact numbers (for example, strong somatic scores with low aspirational scores may suggest a need to focus on future orientation and purpose).

The BWI should never be used to label people as "well enough" or "not well enough." Its purpose is to inform care, not to police access to care.

## Administration and Timing

Who Can Administer

The BWI is designed to be usable across roles, including:

- licensed clinicians

- ECM/case managers and care coordinators

- MSW interns and trainees under supervision

- community health workers and promotoras

- educators and youth leaders

- wellness lab / ARTGard facilitators

No special certification is required, but orientation to the Brain Well-Being Model® and Guard/Healing/Thrive language is recommended so scores are interpreted in context.

Recommended Administration Schedule

- Initial intake / enrollment: Administer once to establish a baseline of wellness and functioning.

- Ongoing services: Every 60–90 days for ECM and case-management clients.

- Wellness labs / ARTGard and community programs: Quarterly or at the beginning and end of a defined group cycle.

- Transitions or changes: After major life stressors, significant care-plan changes, service transitions, or completion of short-term crisis support.

These are guidelines; frequency can be adapted to setting and capacity.

## How the BWI Pairs with Other Tools

The BWI is intended to complement, not replace symptom-based tools.

Common pairing:

- PHQ-9, GAD-7, DASS, or similar → symptom severity

- BWI → functional recovery, regulation, engagement, and hope

Together, these provide a more whole-person picture:

- Is the person's distress decreasing?

- Are they more able to regulate their body, notice and shift their stories, rely on relationships, and stay connected to goals and meaning?

This dual lens is especially important for people and communities whose symptoms remain elevated because environments have not yet changed, but whose BWI scores may show important movement in somatic, relational, or aspirational domains.

## Using BWI Results in Practice

BWI results can be used to:

- Inform care coordination and wellness planning: Identify domains that need more support (for example, strong somatic scores but low relational scores may suggest focusing on connection and support).

- Track progress over time: Notice small movements toward Healing Mode that might not yet show up as major symptom changes.

- Support ECM and CalAIM documentation: Provide brief, structured evidence of functional change and engagement in care.

- Guide non-clinical and clinical engagement strategies: Help CHWs, educators, youth leaders, and clinicians use a shared language to discuss state and needs.

In community spaces like ARTGard, Resilience Studios™, and youth wellness labs, BWI scores can be paired with arts-based tools such as Seeds and Leaves to make movement visible in both numbers and images.

## Guard, Healing, Thrive and the BWI

The Brain Well-Being Model® describes three primary modes—Guard, Healing, and Thrive—that show up in everyday life.

While the BWI does not assign a single "mode score," patterns often reflect movements between modes:

- Predominantly low scores across domains with high strain and little hope may correspond to Guard as baseline.

- Mixed scores (some domains improving, especially somatic and perceptual) often reflect Healing—the nervous system still remembers danger, but it does not run the whole show.

- Higher scores across domains, with stable regulation, connection, and aspiration, align with more time in Thrive—space for creativity, contribution, and shared futures.

Most people and communities move between these modes over time. The BWI helps us notice where they are along this

Stress-to-State Pathway and, more importantly, whether there is movement.

## Protecting the Purpose of the BWI

For the BWI to serve its intended role, systems and practitioners commit to:

- using it to guide support, not to gatekeep or punish people for being in Guard Mode

- interpreting scores through a contextual lens that includes racism, poverty, digital-age stress, and community history

- pairing it with relational conversation, not using it as a standalone number without narrative

When used this way, the Brain Well-Being Index becomes more than a form. It becomes part of a shared language that helps individuals, families, communities, and systems see movement, honor existing strengths, and design environments where safety, connection, and thriving are not rare, but expected.

# Brain Well-Being Index Administration and Use Guidelines

## Purpose of This Appendix

This appendix provides guidance for the safe, ethical, and context-appropriate use of the Brain Well-Being Index™ (BWI) across clinical, educational, community, and public-health environments. Because the BWI is a reflective, non-diagnostic measure of nervous-system state, its administration must prioritize psychological safety, cultural humility, informed participation, and clear role boundaries. The goal of these guidelines is not restriction, but protection—ensuring the BWI remains a tool for awareness and empowerment, never surveillance or judgment.

## Core Orientation for Use

All BWI administration should follow four foundational commitments:

1.  Dignity before data

2. Human experience is always more important than numerical scoring.

3. Safety before insight

4. If reflection increases distress, pause the process and return to regulation.

5. Context before interpretation

6. Scores have meaning only within cultural, relational, developmental, and environmental context.

7. Support before separation

8. The BWI should strengthen connection between people, never isolate or label them.

## Who May Use the BWI

The Brain Well-Being Index™ is intentionally designed for multi-role participation within Collective Care in Action® environments.

Licensed Clinical Professionals

May use the BWI to:

- Support collaborative reflection during care.

- Observe regulation shifts across sessions.

- Complement (not replace) standardized clinical assessment.

- Guide trauma-informed pacing of treatment.

Clinical judgment, mandated-reporting laws, and professional ethics always take precedence over BWI results.

## Community-Based and Non-Clinical Helpers

Including, for example:

- Community health workers (CHWs).

- Doulas and birth workers.

- Educators and school wellness staff.

- Peer supporters.

- Faith and cultural leaders.

- Youth wellness leaders.

These helpers may use the BWI to:

- Facilitate reflective conversations.

- Notice stress and regulation patterns.

- Guide wellness activities and referrals.

- Support shared language around well-being.

Non-clinical users must not present the BWI as diagnosis or treatment.

## Individual and Family Self-Reflection

Individuals, caregivers, and families may use the BWI for:

- Personal awareness of stress and regulation.

- Noticing pre-/post-wellness shifts.

- Family dialogue about emotional states.

- Tracking supportive environments and routines.

Self-use should always emphasize curiosity over self-judgment.

## Settings for Administration

The BWI may be used across diverse environments, including:

- Mental-health and health-care settings.

- Schools and early childhood programs.

- Home-visiting and family-support programs.

- Community wellness labs and outreach events.

- Faith-based and cultural healing spaces.

- Youth leadership and peer-support programs.

- Group workshops and prevention initiatives.

This flexibility reflects a core premise of this work: healing does not live only in clinics.

## Timing of Use

Common administration moments include:

## Reflective Check-In

A brief awareness pause at the beginning of an interaction, session, or activity.

Pre-/Post-Experience Observation

Used before and after:

- Therapeutic sessions.

- Wellness labs.

- Art, movement, or nature-based activities.

- Group circles or community gatherings.

This allows real-time noticing of state shift, the central aim of the BWI.

Ongoing Tracking Over Time

Periodic reflection to observe:

- Regulation trends.

- Changes in relational safety.

- Emerging hope or aspiration.

- Environmental impact on well-being.

Direction of change is more meaningful than any single score.

## Trauma-Informed Administration Practices

To prevent activation of Guard Mode during reflection:

- Offer participation as invitation, never requirement.

- Use gentle, non-clinical language when appropriate.

- Allow verbal, visual, creative, or narrative responses.

- Normalize mixed or fluctuating states.

- Provide regulation support if distress emerges.

- Respect silence or refusal without consequence.

If strong emotional activation occurs, shift immediately to grounding, co-regulation, supportive presence, and clinical referral when indicated. Safety is always the priority.

## Cultural and Community Responsiveness

Ethical BWI use requires attention to:

- Historical mistrust of systems.

- Language accessibility.

- Cultural meaning of emotional expression.

- Community definitions of wellness.

- Power dynamics between helper and participant.

Whenever possible:

- Adapt wording collaboratively.

- Include culturally relevant metaphors or visuals.

- Invite community leadership in implementation.

- Ensure results benefit participants directly.

Measurement without benefit is ethically unacceptable.

## Consent and Transparency

Participants should understand that:

- The BWI is not a diagnosis.

- Participation is voluntary.

- Responses will be used to support well-being, not punish.

- There are limits to confidentiality (especially in clinical or school settings).

- Referral or additional support may be recommended under certain conditions.

Clear explanation builds trust, which is itself regulatory.

## Situations Requiring Clinical Referral

The BWI must never delay access to professional care. Immediate referral is required when there are indications of:

- Suicidal ideation or self-harm risk.

- Danger to others.

- Abuse or neglect.

- Severe functional impairment.

- Psychosis or medical instability.

- Acute trauma exposure without support.

In these cases, follow:

- Mandated-reporting laws.

- Organizational protocols.

- Clinical supervision procedures.

- Emergency response pathways.

The BWI is a supportive reflection tool, not a crisis instrument.

## Documentation and Data Use

When BWI information is recorded:

- Store data securely according to setting regulations.

- Avoid stigmatizing language in notes.

- Document context, not just scores.

- Use aggregate data only for healing-aligned evaluation.

- Ensure communities benefit from findings (for example, through shared summaries, co-interpretation, or co-design of next steps).

Ethical measurement redistributes knowledge back to the people who generated it.

## Boundaries of the Tool

The Brain Well-Being Index does not:

- Diagnose mental illness.

- Determine eligibility for services.

- Replace clinical screening tools.

- Predict risk with certainty.

- Measure the full complexity of healing.

Its function is narrower and more humane: to help people notice when safety, connection, and hope are changing.

## Closing Guidance

The integrity of the Brain Well-Being Index does not live in the form itself. It lives in how it is held by the people using it.

When administered with:

- Humility.

- Cultural respect.

- Relational safety.

- Ethical clarity.

- Genuine care.

the BWI becomes more than a measurement tool. It becomes a shared language of healing—one capable of moving across clinics, classrooms, homes, and communities without losing dignity. And in environments where people have long been measured only by what is wrong, that shift alone can begin to restore trust.

# Brain Well-Being Index Scoring, Interpretation, and Clinical Integration

## Purpose of This Appendix

This appendix outlines the scoring structure, interpretation guidance, and responsible integration of the Brain Well-Being Index (BWI) within clinical, educational, community, and public-health settings. Because the BWI is a reflective, non-diagnostic measure of nervous-system state, its scoring system is intentionally simple, trauma-informed, and adaptable across environments. The purpose of scoring is not classification, but clarity—helping individuals and helpers notice patterns of regulation, connection, and emerging hope over time.

## I. Structure of the Brain Well-Being Index

The BWI reflects lived experience across the four awareness domains of the Brain Well-Being Model®:

- Somatic Awareness

- Body-based experience of safety or strain (for example, tension, breath, sleep, appetite, pain, numbness, energy).

- Perceptual Awareness

- How reality is interpreted (threat-focused, neutral, or possibility-oriented perception).

- Relational Awareness

- Capacity for trust, connection, belonging, and co-regulation.

- Aspirational Awareness

- Future orientation, meaning, purpose, imagination, and hope.

Each domain represents a distinct but interdependent pathway of healing. Movement in any single domain may influence the others.

## II. Scoring Continuum

Each domain is rated along a five-point state continuum:

- 0 — Guard Dominant

  Persistent survival activation; minimal access to regulation or connection.

- 1 — High Strain

Frequent distress; brief or inconsistent regulation; limited relational safety.

- 2 — Transitional / Mixed State

Fluctuation between Guard and regulation; moments of safety emerging.

- 3 — Regulating

Increasing stability, relational access, and emotional flexibility.

- 4 — Thrive Accessible

Consistent access to safety, connection, purpose, creativity, and joy (not permanent thriving, but reliable return).

**Key principles of scoring**

- Scores represent current state, not identity.

- Movement of even one point is biologically meaningful.

- Direction over time matters more than any single number.

- Mixed or uneven domain scores are normal in healing.

- No score is "bad"; all scores provide information for care.

# III. Methods of Rating

The BWI may be completed through multiple reflective formats, depending on context and role.

1. Self-Reflection Rating

Individuals rate their own experience using:

- Numeric scale (0–4).

- Visual scale (colors, faces, symbols).

- Narrative description.

- Creative expression (drawing, metaphor, movement).

Self-rating centers autonomy and lived experience.

2. Collaborative Reflection

Helper and participant co-notice state together through dialogue:

- "What feels most true in your body today?"

- "Do things feel mostly unsafe, mixed, or more steady?"

- "Is hope closer, farther, or unchanged?"

This approach prioritizes relationship over measurement.

3. Observational Clinical Use

Licensed professionals may integrate:

- Behavioral observation.

- Affect-regulation patterns.

- Relational engagement.

- Functional stability.

Observation must remain tentative and collaborative, never imposed as absolute truth.

## IV. Interpreting Domain Patterns

Guard-Dominant Profile

(majority scores 0–1)

May indicate:

- High survival activation.

- Limited access to regulation.

- Relational mistrust or withdrawal.

- Reduced future orientation.

Primary focus: safety, stabilization, co-regulation, and environmental support—not insight-oriented processing.

Transitional Profile

(majority scores near 2)

May indicate:

- Emerging regulation.

- Fluctuating safety.

- Partial relational openness.

- Inconsistent hope.

Primary focus: repetition of safe experiences, relational consistency, and gentle skill-building.

Regulating / Thrive-Accessing Profile

(majority scores 3–4)

May indicate:

- More stable regulation.

- Relational engagement.

- Future orientation.

- Adaptive flexibility.

Primary focus: purpose development, leadership, contribution, and sustaining environments of care.

## V. Using Change Over Time

The most meaningful BWI information comes from observing change, not single scores.

## Pre- / Post-Experience Reflection

For example:

- Before a therapy session, wellness lab, group circle, art, movement, or nature-based activity.

- After the experience.

Even micro-shifts (for example, Somatic 1 → 2) indicate that nervous-system learning is occurring.

## Longitudinal Tracking

Used to observe:

- Recovery trends.

- Relapse patterns.

- Environmental impact.

- Effectiveness of interventions.

- Community-level change in aggregate data.

Longitudinal use must remain non-punitive and dignity-centered.

## VI. Clinical Integration Guidelines

The BWI Complements—Not Replaces—Clinical Assessment

Licensed professionals may use the BWI alongside:

- Diagnostic evaluation.

- Risk assessment.

- Standardized symptom measures.

- Treatment planning and review.

The BWI uniquely contributes:

- State awareness (Guard / Healing / Thrive).

- Relational and environmental context.

- Regulation tracking.

- Hope and aspirational awareness.

These are areas often missed by symptom-only tools.

## Treatment Planning Applications

BWI patterns may help guide emphasis:

- Guard-Dominant

- Stabilization, safety planning, somatic regulation, environmental support, and strengthening basic relational safety.

- Transitional

- Skill-building, relational repair, gradual trauma processing, and consistent co-regulation.

- Regulating / Thrive-Accessing

- Identity development, leadership roles, community engagement, and prevention-focused work.

Documentation Language (Recommended)

Use non-pathologizing phrasing, such as:

- "Participant reports increased access to regulation."

- "Relational safety appears more consistent than previous session."

- "Aspirational awareness is emerging following community engagement."

Avoid language that labels people based solely on scores (for example, "client is a '2'").

## VII. Community and Population-Level Interpretation

When aggregated ethically, BWI data may help systems:

- Identify unmet regulation needs.

- Evaluate wellness programming.

- Track prevention impact.

- Guide resource allocation.

- Document health-equity outcomes.

A critical safeguard: community data must benefit the community, not simply inform institutions. Aggregate findings should be shared back in accessible ways and used to co-design next steps with community members.

## VIII. Limitations of the BWI

The Brain Well-Being Index:

- Is not diagnostic.

- Cannot determine mental illness.

- Cannot replace clinical judgment.

- Cannot predict a crisis with certainty.

- Does not capture the full depth of culture or story.

Its role is intentionally modest: to make shifts in safety, connection, and hope more visible.

## IX. Ethical Integration Across Systems

Responsible use requires:

- Trauma-informed training.

- Cultural humility.

- Informed consent.

- Confidentiality protection.

- Clear referral pathways.

- Prohibition of punitive or exclusionary use.

Any use that harms dignity or restricts access to support violates the purpose of the BWI.

## X. Closing Integration

Scoring systems in mental health have historically focused on symptoms, risk, deficits, and dysfunction. The Brain Well-Being Index introduces a different measurement question: Where is life beginning to return?

When used with care, the BWI does more than track distress. It documents:

- Regulation appearing.

- Connection strengthening.

- Hope re-entering.

- Communities healing.

In systems that have long measured only what is broken, learning to measure what is growing is itself a form of repair.

# Seeds and Leaves Practice Guides

## Purpose of This Appendix

This appendix offers practical guidance for using Seeds and Leaves as everyday tools for nervous-system awareness and collective reflection. These practices are simple by design so they can move easily between homes, schools, Resilience Studios™, clinics, and community spaces without requiring special equipment or advanced training.

Seeds and Leaves are not tests or behavior charts. They are invitations to notice how we arrive, how we leave, and what changes—if anything—in between.

## Seeds: Naming How We Arrive

Seeds are quick check-ins that ask a simple question: *How am I arriving right now?* They can be used with children, youth, and adults.

What Seeds Can Look Like

Seeds can take many forms:

- Small cards with abstract images, colors, or shapes.

- Blank circles or "seed" outlines people can draw or write in.

- A simple word list (for example, tense, numb, hopeful, tired, buzzing).

- Digital icons or emojis when used online.

The exact format matters less than the intention: to give people a low-pressure way to express how their body and story are coming into the space.

How to Use Seeds

In families and households

- Place Seeds cards on a table, counter, or wall where people pass regularly.

- Invite family members to choose or draw a Seed at predictable times (for example, morning, after school, before bed).

- Ask short, open questions: "Which Seed feels like you right now?" or "What made you choose that one?"

In classrooms and youth programs

- Offer Seeds at the door or on desks as students arrive.

- Use a brief whole-group check-in: "Who is arriving with a stormy Seed today? Who is arriving more calm?"

- Allow students to pass or share only what feels safe; no one should be forced to explain.

In Resilience Studios™, groups, and sessions

- Start groups with a Seeds moment to help facilitators gauge collective Guard / Healing / Thrive.

- Use Seeds to notice patterns (for example, certain days or activities where Guard is high).

- Invite staff to participate alongside participants so nervous-system literacy is shared.

Practice Principles for Seeds

- Keep it optional; invitation, not requirement.

- Keep it brief; Seeds are not intended to become long therapy sessions.

- Normalize all Seeds; Guard-like Seeds are not "bad," Thrive-like Seeds are not "good."

- Let Seeds inform your pacing, tone, and expectations for the time together.

## Leaves: Noticing What Has Shifted

Leaves are reflections on what, if anything, feels different after an experience. They ask: *What changed for you—even a little—while you were here?*

What Leaves Can Look Like

Leaves can take forms such as:

- Small cards in the shape of leaves.

- Blank "leaf" outlines to draw or write in.

- Simple prompts like "One thing that feels a bit different now is…"

- Digital sticky notes or comments for online groups.

Leaves are about change, not performance. "No change" is an acceptable and important answer.

## How to Use Leaves

*In families and households*

- At the end of the day or week, invite each person to add a Leaf to a shared "tree" on the wall.

- Prompts might include: "Something my body did this week that I'm proud of," "A moment I felt safer," or "Something that stayed the same."

- Periodically step back and look at the tree together to remember small shifts.

*In classrooms and youth programs*

- Use Leaves at the end of lessons, projects, or circles.

- Ask what felt different from the beginning to the end (energy, focus, connection, mood).

- Create a visible Leaves display so students can see growth over time, especially in spaces where they often feel only evaluated.

- Close with Leaves to help participants and staff name even micro-shifts in somatic, relational, or aspirational awareness.

- Invite statements like "I feel the same," "My shoulders dropped a little," "I feel more connected," or "I remembered something I care about."

- Include staff Leaves alongside participant Leaves to honor everyone's nervous systems.

## Practice Principles for Leaves

- Honor honesty; "tired," "still angry," or "no change" are valid Leaves.

- Avoid turning Leaves into a satisfaction survey; they are about experience, not ratings.

- Look for patterns in Leaves to understand what genuinely supports regulation and connection in your setting.

- Use Leaves to guide design: if many people report more hope or ease after certain activities, protect those practices.

## Putting Seeds and Leaves Together

Used together, Seeds and Leaves create a simple arc:

- Seed: How am I arriving?

- Experience: What happens in this space (class, session, visit, gathering)?

- Leaf: What feels different now, if anything?

Over time, this arc teaches individuals and communities to notice:

- Which environments consistently pull them into Guard Mode.

- Which relationships and practices reliably move them toward Healing or Thrive.

- How small, repeated experiences of safety and connection accumulate.

This noticing is a core part of Collective Care in Action®. It gives people language and evidence for what helps them feel a bit more human in systems that have often reduced them to numbers or "compliance."

## Adaptation and Cultural Honoring

Seeds and Leaves are meant to be adapted:

- Use images, colors, and metaphors that reflect local culture and community wisdom.

- Translate prompts into preferred languages and dialects.

- Invite youth, elders, and cultural leaders to help design Seeds and Leaves that feel like they belong to the community, not just to a program.

The question to keep returning to is simple: *Does this practice help people feel safer, more seen, and more hopeful?* If yes, it is aligned with the spirit of this work—even if the Seeds and Leaves do not look exactly like the examples here.

# F.L.O.W.S. Framework for Everyday Practice

## Purpose of This Appendix

This appendix summarizes the F.L.O.W.S. framework as a practical tool for everyday regulation and reflection. F.L.O.W.S. is designed to be simple enough for use in homes, classrooms, Resilience Studios™, clinics, and community settings, while still honoring the complexity of nervous-system experience.

F.L.O.W.S. is not a protocol for emergencies or a substitute for treatment. It is a way to create a small pocket of space between activation and action—space where care, choice, and connection can return.

## The F.L.O.W.S. Sequence

F — Feel

Notice what is happening in your body right now.

- Ask: "What sensations am I aware of?"

- Examples: tight chest, racing heart, clenched jaw, shaky hands, heavy limbs, numbness, buzzing energy.

- There is nothing to fix at this step. The goal is simply to notice.

## L — Locate

Identify where in your body the sensation is most present.

- Ask: "Where do I feel this the most?"

- Examples: "In my stomach," "in my shoulders," "behind my eyes," "in my throat."

- Locating turns a vague storm into something more specific and manageable.

## O — Open

Create a little more room around the sensation.

- Ask: "What could help this area soften or have a bit more space?"

- Examples: taking three slower breaths, loosening your jaw, dropping your shoulders, uncurling your hands, changing posture, stepping outside, drinking water, stretching.

- Opening does not mean erasing the feeling. It means reducing the pressure enough that you are not fully in Guard Mode.

## W — Witness

Notice the story your mind is telling about what is happening.

- Ask: "What is the narrative in my head right now?"

- Examples: "They don't respect me," "I always mess this up," "We're not safe here," "I have to handle everything."

- You do not have to argue with the story. Simply recognizing, "This is what my Guard Mode is saying," helps create a small separation between story and self.

**S — Shift**

Choose one small, realistic action that supports Healing or Thrive.

- Ask: "Given what I'm feeling and noticing, what is one kind step I can take?"

- Examples: asking for a pause, sending a text for support, changing the order of tasks, saying "I need five minutes," drinking water, moving to a quieter space, scheduling a fuller conversation for later instead of right now.

- The shift is not the whole solution. It is the next doable move toward safety, connection, or clarity.

## Using F.L.O.W.S. in Different Contexts

*For individuals*

- In the car after a hard appointment or school meeting.

- At home when you notice yourself about to yell, shut down, or over-function.

- Before answering a difficult email or message.

*For families and caregivers*

- Pausing to use F.L.O.W.S. yourself before responding to a child or teen in Guard Mode.

- Modeling out loud in simple language: "My chest is tight (Feel), it's right here (Locate), I'm going to take a breath (Open), my brain is saying you don't care (Witness), I'm going to ask for a minute before we keep talking (Shift)."

- Using a simplified version with children ("body check, where is it, one small help").

*For teams and organizations*

- Beginning or ending supervision and debrief conversations with a brief F.L.O.W.S. check.

- Using F.L.O.W.S. after critical incidents to focus not only on events and tasks, but also on what staff carried in their bodies and what they need next.

- Encouraging leaders to model F.L.O.W.S. publicly so regulation is treated as shared work, not a private deficit.

*For groups and community spaces*

- Teaching a youth-friendly version (for example, Feel–Find–Breathe–Notice–Do One Thing) in circles and programs.

- Integrating very short F.L.O.W.S. pauses into Resilience Studio™ activities, workshops, or faith gatherings.

- Using the framework to normalize talking about Guard / Healing / Thrive without shaming anyone for where they are.

## Practice Considerations

- F.L.O.W.S. is meant to be gentle. If at any point it increases distress, return to simpler grounding (breath, movement, sensory focus) and, when needed, seek professional support.

- F.L.O.W.S. should never be used to pressure people to "calm down" for the comfort of others. Its purpose is to support the person's own nervous system and agency.

- Over time, repeated use of F.L.O.W.S. can help individuals and communities recognize their early Guard signals and respond with more care rather than automatic reaction.

The central question is not "Did we do F.L.O.W.S. perfectly?" but "Are we creating more moments where bodies, stories, and relationships have room to move from Guard toward Healing and Thrive?"

# Everyday Collective Care Practices

## Purpose of This Appendix

This appendix offers a practical menu of everyday practices that bring the Brain Well-Being Model® and Collective Care in Action® into daily life. It is written for caregivers, community health workers, educators, youth leaders, faith leaders, and organizational teams who want simple, repeatable ways to support regulation, belonging, and hope in real-world settings.

These examples are not prescriptions. They are starting points you can adapt to your own community, culture, spiritual traditions, and capacity. You are encouraged to choose a few practices that feel realistic, repeat them consistently, and allow them to evolve over time in collaboration with the people you serve.

## 1. Home and Family Micro-Practices

- Five-Minute Regulation Ritual

  Choose one small daily ritual—before school, after work, or before bed—where each person pauses to notice their body (somatic), name one feeling or thought (perceptual), share it with a trusted person (relational), and name one small hope or intention for the next day (aspirational).

- Seeds and Leaves Wall

  Create a simple wall or board where family members can post "Seeds" (how I am arriving, what I am carrying) and "Leaves" (small moments of growth, courage, or rest). Over time, this becomes a living record that survival is not the whole story.

- Guard Mode Check-In for Caregivers

  Once a week, caregivers take five minutes to ask: Where did my Guard Mode show up this week? What helped it soften, even a little? What support do I need to feel one percent safer in my own body and life?

## 2. Classroom and School Practices

- Nervous-System Literacy Moments

  Integrate a brief shared language into the school day—such as "Guard Mode," "Healing Mode," and "Thrive Mode"—so students and staff can name, without shame, how their nervous systems are arriving and what they might need to shift.

- Predictable Openings and Closings

  Begin and end classes with the same brief rituals (a grounding breath, a song, a question of the day, a gratitude round). Predictability reduces allostatic load and helps students' bodies know what to expect.

- Regulation Stations

  Create small, low-cost regulation corners with fidgets, art materials, sensory items, or reflection prompts. These spaces normalize taking a brief regulation break, not as punishment, but as nervous-system care.

## 3. Community Health Worker and Peer Practices

- Mode Check at the Door

  Before group sessions, CHWs and peer specialists can invite participants to quietly choose which mode they feel closest to—Guard, Healing, or Thrive—through color cards, symbols, or a simple gesture. This guides pace, depth, and expectations for the session.

- F.L.O.W.S. in the Field

  CHWs can use the F.L.O.W.S. framework as a portable tool: helping people Feel what is present, Listen to their inner story, Open a bit of space, connect With someone or something supportive, and Step into one tiny action that supports safety.

- Shared Boundaries as Practice

  Teams name, out loud, one boundary for their day or week (for example, "no new intakes after 3 p.m." or "at least a 10-minute break between high-intensity visits"). This models that boundaries are part of collective care, not personal failure.

# 4. Faith, Cultural, and Spiritual Spaces

- Rituals as Regulation

  Faith leaders and cultural healers can intentionally frame existing rituals—song, prayer, drumming, communal meals, anointing, meditation—as somatic and relational practices that help nervous systems move from Guard toward Healing Mode.

- Healing Circles and Testimony as Collective Care

  Story-sharing spaces, testimony, and healing circles can be gently structured to include grounding at the beginning, a clear closing, and an invitation to name not only pain but also moments of care, creativity, and divine or ancestral support.

- Sanctuary as Resilience Studio™

  Faith and cultural spaces can see themselves as Resilience Studios™: designing lighting, sound, seating, and flow with nervous-system safety in mind, and pairing spiritual care with practical resources such as food, housing support, or CHW connection.

# 5. Organizational and Workforce Practices

- Regulation-First Team Meetings

  Begin staff meetings with two to three minutes of regulation (breath, stretching, brief silence, a check-in question) before moving into agenda items. This honors that people are bodies in systems, not just roles in an organization.

- Collective Efficacy Boards

  Maintain a visible shared board or digital space where staff record small wins: a conflict de-escalated, a student re-engaged, a family supported, a system barrier reduced. This reinforces the belief that "we can act together," a critical ingredient of hope.

- Reflective Supervision as Collective Care

  Supervisors integrate questions like: Where is Guard Mode showing up in our team? What do we need to feel safer, more supported, and more human at work? This invites healing at the organizational nervous-system level, not only the individual.

## Closing Reflection

Everyday collective care is not about perfect programs. It is about repeated, accessible practices that tell nervous systems: you are not alone here, you are allowed to rest, and your healing is connected to ours. Even the smallest shared ritual can become a seed of cultural change.

# Implementation and Partner Notes

**Purpose of This Appendix**

This appendix is for practitioners, organizations, and systems leaders who want to bring the Brain Well-Being Model®, the Brain Well-Being Index (BWI), and Collective Care in Action® into practice. It offers high-level guidance for implementation, not a rigid manual. Every community will adapt these ideas differently; what matters most is that implementation increases safety, dignity, and belonging.

The goal is to align policies, environments, and workforce practices with nervous-system science and community wisdom so that prevention, regulation, and collective care become part of everyday infrastructure rather than temporary projects.

## 1. Guiding Principles for Implementation

### Relationship Before Tool

The Brain Well-Being Index and related practices should always be grounded in genuine relationship, consent, and trust. Tools are most effective when people feel seen, not surveilled.

### Co-Design With Communities

Involve youth, caregivers, elders, frontline staff, and community leaders from the beginning. Treat lived experience and cultural knowledge as equal to technical expertise, and ask regularly: Does this feel like it belongs to us, or like something being done to us?

## Start Small and Build Rhythms

Choose a few practices you can sustain, such as Seeds and Leaves in groups, F.L.O.W.S. in supervision, or BWI reflections in one program. Focus on consistency over complexity; repeated, simple rhythms shape nervous systems more than one-time events.

## Align, Don't Compete, With Existing Efforts

Connect the Brain Well-Being Model® to work already underway, such as trauma-informed practice, SEL, restorative justice, health-equity initiatives, CalAIM, and Community Supports. Use the four domains—somatic, perceptual, relational, and aspirational—as a bridge across frameworks, roles, and departments.

## Protect Workforce as Infrastructure

Recognize that staff nervous systems are part of the intervention. Build in structures for regulation, reflection, repair, and sustainability for helpers, not only expectations for productivity.

## Cultural and Spiritual Intelligence

Implementation must honor cultural traditions, language, and spiritual practices already functioning as healing in a community. The model is meant to sit beside, not above, existing wisdom.

## Do No Additional Harm

Any use of this framework should decrease stigma and shame,

not increase them. Data, stories, and evaluation must be used to support communities, not to police or punish them.

# 2. Implementation Pathways Across Systems

## Schools and Youth Programs

Early steps include introducing Guard Mode, Healing Mode, and Thrive Mode to staff first, with space for them to reflect on their own nervous systems; integrating Seeds at arrival and Leaves at closing in a small pilot group, such as one grade level or one after-school program; and using F.L.O.W.S. as a staff tool in debriefs before teaching it to students.

As the work grows, schools can add simple somatic practices to classroom routines, use BWI snapshots where appropriate and consented to understand how students experience somatic, relational, and aspirational safety, and align discipline practices with nervous-system science by focusing more on regulation, relationships, and repair than on punishment alone.

## Clinics, Plans, and Community Health

Early steps include orienting clinical staff, CHWs, and front-desk teams to the Brain Well-Being Model® and Collective Care in Action®; using Seeds and Leaves informally in waiting areas or groups to learn how people are arriving and leaving; and introducing F.L.O.W.S. into supervision and case consultations.

Over time, sites can integrate the BWI as a reflective tool in selected programs with clear consent and follow-up pathways, align care coordination and benefits with the four domains of awareness, and treat CHWs, doulas, and peer specialists as regulatory infrastructure rather than add-ons to referral systems.

**Community-Based Organizations and Resilience StudiosTM**
Organizations can begin by reviewing current programming through the four domains of awareness, asking where somatic, perceptual, relational, and aspirational support are already present and where the gaps are. They can add Seeds and Leaves to groups, circles, and events, and normalize staff naming their own Guard, Healing, or Thrive mode in team spaces.

As implementation deepens, organizations can develop ARTGard-style spaces, play-based and creative healing practices, use aggregate BWI reflections to co-design offerings with participants rather than guessing needs, and build partnerships with schools, clinics, and plans so Resilience StudiosTM are recognized as part of the local healing ecosystem.

**Faith and Cultural Institutions**
Partner with faith leaders, cultural healers, and trusted community figures to adapt language and practices so they resonate with local theology, cosmology, ritual, and cultural narratives of resilience. Implementation in these settings should honor spiritual and cultural traditions already functioning as healing in the community.

# 3. Working with Partners and Systems

**Building Shared Language**
Offer short, accessible orientations to schools, clinics, funders, and plan partners that introduce Guard/Healing/Thrive, the four domains of awareness, and simple examples of Seeds and Leaves, F.L.O.W.S., and the BWI. Invite partners to identify where they already see these ideas in their work rather than framing implementation as starting from zero.

**Aligning Metrics With Lived Experience**

When possible, pair existing metrics such as attendance, utilization, hospitalizations, and suspensions with BWI-informed reflections and qualitative stories. These combined data should help partners ask better design questions, not assign blame to individuals or communities.

**Sustaining the Work**

Identify champions across settings—youth, staff, leaders, and community partners—who care about nervous-system-informed, culturally intelligent care. Build communities of practice where they can learn from one another, share missteps, and refine tools over time.

# 4. Roles and Responsibilities of Partners

**Community Health Workers, Peers, and Frontline Staff**

Carry nervous-system literacy into homes, schools, shelters, clinics, and neighborhoods; facilitate groups; support BWI reflections; and provide feedback on what is realistic, culturally resonant, and effective.

**Organizational Leaders**

Create policies, schedules, and environments that support staff regulation and sustainability. Protect time for training, reflection, debrief, and collaborative problem-solving.

**Funders and Policy Partners**

Resource prevention, workforce development, reflective supervision, and evaluation efforts. Support flexible funding that allows communities to adapt the model to their realities rather than forcing a single template.

# 5. Ethical Use of the Brain Well-Being Index

### Voluntary and Informed Use
Participation in BWI reflections should be voluntary, with clear explanation of purpose, how information will be used, and how it will not be used.

### Strengths-Oriented Framing
Emphasize that the BWI tracks shifts in state, not pathology or worth. Focus on growth, direction, and what supports movement toward Healing and Thrive Modes.

### Data Stewardship and Feedback
When BWI or related data are collected, communities should see the results in clear, accessible ways and help interpret what they mean. Data should support advocacy, resource allocation, and improved care—not extract value from communities.

# 6. Stages of Implementation

### Stage 1: Exploration and Relationship-Building
Listen to what communities and staff are already doing to support regulation and collective care. Identify natural alignment points, existing wisdom, and potential risks.

### Stage 2: Training and Pilots
Offer training in the Brain Well-Being Model®, Collective Care in Action®, and the BWI. Start with small pilots in willing sites, with clear feedback loops and room to adapt.

### Stage 3: Integration and Scaling
Integrate the model into organizational practices, supervision, policies, space design, and funding structures where it is

working well. Support cross-site learning communities so practitioners can share adaptations and lessons learned.

### Stage 4: Evaluation and Continuous Learning

Pair implementation with reflective evaluation, including both quantitative and qualitative data. Adjust practices in response to what participants, staff, and partners say and experience.

# 7. Training and Support

When considering training and technical assistance, look for support that includes both content and container: the model, tools, and science, as well as safety, reflection, and cultural responsiveness. Prioritize trainers who understand both practice and systems change, and make sure there is a plan for ongoing support such as coaching, peer learning, or communities of practice rather than one-time workshops alone.

### Innovative Wellness Consulting

Innovative Wellness Consulting (IWC) offers training, consultation, and implementation support rooted in the Brain Well-Being Model® and Collective Care in Action®. IWC partners with schools, community-based organizations, health systems, and faith- and culture-based groups to design enriched environments, Resilience Studios™, and workforce trainings that build nervous-system literacy, regulation skills, and collective care practices into everyday life.

Training options may include introductory Brain Well-Being Model® overviews, facilitator and CHW/peer trainings, ARTGard and Resilience Studio™ implementation support, and customized coaching or communities of practice for leaders and teams integrating this work into policy, programs, and direct service.

Contact Innovative Wellness Consulting for training opportunities:

Email: hello@iwc-ca.com

Website: https://www.iwc-ca.com

# 8. Partnership With Public Policy and Systems Change

Implementation is most sustainable when it is aligned with larger policy movements toward trauma-informed care, social-determinants integration, community health worker expansion, school-based prevention, and value-based payment. When possible, partners can:

- Advocate for reimbursement of community-rooted healing work, including CHWs, peers, doulas, and youth leaders.
- Integrate Brain Well-Being measures and language into prevention, equity, and innovation initiatives.
- Use findings from local implementation to inform city, county, state, or national policy decisions.

## Closing Note on Implementation

The Brain Well-Being Model® and Collective Care in Action® are not meant to be imposed on communities from the outside. They are meant to name, support, and strengthen what many families, healers, and organizers have practiced for generations: safety, connection, and shared responsibility for one another's lives.

Implementation is not about perfect fidelity to a script. It is about alignment with core values: dignity before data, safety before insight, context before interpretation, and support before separation. When those values guide how this framework is brought into a setting, healing can become more visible, more coordinated, and more possible—so that it is no longer the exception, but part of the environment communities are building together.

# Scholarly References and Evidence Base

*Scientific Foundations of the Brain Well-Being Model® and Collective Care in Action®*

## Purpose of This Appendix

This appendix presents the interdisciplinary scientific and scholarly foundations informing the theoretical, clinical, and public-health architecture of the Brain Well-Being Model® and Collective Care in Action®.

The evidence base spans:

- neuroscience and stress physiology

- attachment and relational development

- trauma and adversity research

- play therapy and experiential healing

- systems-based compassion and organizational regulation

- public health equity and social determinants of health

- workforce-based, community-rooted care models

Together, these fields converge around a central insight: human nervous systems develop, adapt, and heal within relational and environmental contexts, and sustainable mental well-being cannot be separated from the systems in which people live.

## I. Neuroscience, Trauma, and Stress Physiology

American Academy of Pediatrics. (2021). Trauma-informed care in child health systems. *Pediatrics, 148*(2), e2021052579.

Bush, N. R., Sullivan, A. D. W., Norona-Zhou, A., et al. (2025). Early life stress effects on children's biology, behavior, and health: Evidence, mediators, moderators, and solutions. *Annual Review of Psychology*.

Centers for Disease Control and Prevention. (2022–2024). Adverse childhood experiences (ACEs) prevention resources.

Centers for Disease Control and Prevention. (2023). Maternal mortality and racial disparities in the United States.

Hughes, K., Bellis, M. A., Hardcastle, K. A., et al. (2017). The effect of multiple adverse childhood experiences on health: A systematic review and meta-analysis. *The Lancet Public Health, 2*(8), e356–e366.

McEwen, B. S. (1998). Protective and damaging effects of stress mediators. *New England Journal of Medicine, 338*(3), 171–179.

National Scientific Council on the Developing Child. (2014). *Excessive stress disrupts the architecture of the developing brain* (Working Paper 3, updated ed.). Harvard University / Center on the Developing Child.

Shonkoff, J. P., & Garner, A. S. (2012). The lifelong effects of early childhood adversity and toxic stress. *Pediatrics, 129*(1), e232–e246.

Siegel, D. J. (2012). *The developing mind* (2nd ed.). Guilford Press.

Suzuki, W. (2021). *Good anxiety: Harnessing the power of the most misunderstood emotion.* Atria Books.

## II. Attachment, Relational Neurobiology, and Radical Empathy

Ainsworth, M. D. S., Blehar, M. C., Waters, E., & Wall, S. (1978). *Patterns of attachment: A psychological study of the strange situation.* Erlbaum.

Bowlby, J. (1982). *Attachment and loss: Vol. 1. Attachment* (2nd ed.). Basic Books. (Original work published 1969)

Ferenczi, S. (1988). Confusion of tongues between adults and the child. In *Final contributions to the problems and methods of psychoanalysis* (pp. 156–167). Karnac. (Original work published 1932)

Porges, S. W. (2011). *The polyvagal theory: Neurophysiological foundations of emotions, attachment, communication, and self-regulation.* W. W. Norton.

Schore, A. N. (2003). *Affect dysregulation and disorders of the self.* W. W. Norton.

Zero To Three. (2022–2024). Infant and early childhood mental health resources.

This body of work informs the model's understanding of safety, relational repair, and the neurobiological foundations of radical empathy.

## III. Play Therapy, Experiential Healing, and Structured Relational Models

Blaustein, M. E., & Kinniburgh, K. M. (2018). *Treating traumatic stress in children and adolescents: How to foster resilience through attachment, self-regulation, and competency.* Guilford Press.

Booth, P. B., & Jernberg, A. M. (2010). *Theraplay: Helping parents and children build better relationships through attachment-based play.* Jossey-Bass.

Landreth, G. L. (2012). *Play therapy: The art of the relationship* (3rd ed.). Routledge.

Malchiodi, C. A. (2015). *Creative interventions with traumatized children.* Guilford Press.

Oaklander, V. (1988). *Windows to our children: A Gestalt therapy approach to children and adolescents.* Gestalt Journal Press.

Van der Kolk, B. A. (2014). *The body keeps the score: Brain, mind, and body in the healing of trauma.* Viking.

These models translate attachment science into structured relational practice and inform the practical architecture of co-regulation within the Brain Well-Being Model®.

## IV. Compassionate Systems and Institutional Regulation

Center for Systems Awareness. (n.d.). *Compassionate Systems Framework.*

Senge, P., Hamilton, H., & Kania, J. (2015). The dawn of system leadership. *Stanford Social Innovation Review, 13*(1), 27–33.

Compassionate systems work reframes leadership and institutional design as regulatory forces, influencing collective stress, belonging, and resilience, and informs the systems-level application of the Brain Well-Being Model®.

## V. Public Health, Health Equity, and Social Determinants

Aspen Institute Ascend. (2025). *The 2Gen investment case: Making the most of capital in all its forms.* Aspen Institute.

Center for Health Care Strategies. (2023). *Coordinating Medicaid health-related social services through community care hubs.*

Collaborative for Academic, Social, and Emotional Learning (CASEL). (2020). *CASEL SEL framework.*

JAMA Network Open. (2023). Racial disparities in mortality and health outcomes in the United States. *JAMA Network Open.*

Kaiser Family Foundation. (2023). *Racial disparities in health outcomes and access to care.*

Los Angeles County Department of Public Health. (2023–2025). *State of Black Los Angeles County* (Reports and trend analyses).

National Academies of Sciences, Engineering, and Medicine. (2019). *Integrating social care into the delivery of health care: Moving upstream to improve the nation's health*. National Academies Press.

World Health Organization. (2022). *World mental health report: Transforming mental health for all*.

These sources ground the model's emphasis on structural determinants, collective trauma, and the integration of social care within health systems.

## VI. Emerging Prevention and Workforce-Based Care Models

California Department of Health Care Services. (2022–2024). *CalAIM Enhanced Care Management and Community Supports guidance*.

Centers for Medicare & Medicaid Services. (2023). *Coverage of health-related social needs (HRSN) services in Medicaid and CHIP* (State Health Official Letter).

Substance Abuse and Mental Health Services Administration. (2020). *National guidelines for behavioral health crisis care: Best practice toolkit*.

U.S. Surgeon General. (2021). *Protecting youth mental health: The U.S. Surgeon General's advisory*.

These frameworks support the model's application within workforce development, care coordination, and preventive, community-based mental health systems.

## VII. Black Literary Lineage and Collective Care Imagination

Angelou, M. (2009). *I know why the caged bird sings*. Random House. (Original work published 1969)

Baldwin, J. (1963). *The fire next time*. Dial Press.

Coates, T.-N. (2015). *Between the world and me*. Spiegel & Grau.

hooks, b. (2000). *All about love: New visions*. William Morrow.

Menakem, R. (2017). *My grandmother's hands: Racialized trauma and the pathway to mending our hearts and bodies*. Central Recovery Press.

These works offer narrative, ethical, and somatic insights into Black survival, love, and intergenerational trauma, deepening the model's application to Black America and to Black Los Angeles in particular.

## Closing Note on Evidence and Lineage

The Brain Well-Being Model® and Collective Care in Action® are not derived from a single discipline. They emerge from the convergence of early relational psychoanalytic insight, attachment science, polyvagal-informed neurobiology, structured relational trauma interventions, compassionate systems leadership, public health equity research, community-rooted healing traditions, and Black literary and cultural lineages naming trauma, love, and survival.

Together, these fields affirm a central conclusion: mental health cannot be fully understood—or sustainably healed—outside the relational, cultural, and systemic environments in which people live.

For a narrative overview of how these traditions come together in this text, see the Foundational Clinical and Cultural Lineage section.

# References


Ainsworth, M. D. S., Blehar, M. C., Waters, E., & Wall, S. (1978). *Patterns of attachment: A psychological study of the strange situation.* Erlbaum.

American Academy of Pediatrics. (2021). Trauma-informed care in child health systems. *Pediatrics, 148*(2), e2021052579.

Angelou, M. (2009). *I know why the caged bird sings.* Random House.

Aspen Institute Ascend. (2025). *The 2Gen investment case: Making the most of capital in all its forms.* Aspen Institute.

Baldwin, J. (1963). *The fire next time.* Dial Press.

Blaustein, M. E., & Kinniburgh, K. M. (2018). *Treating traumatic stress in children and adolescents: How to foster resilience through attachment, self-regulation, and competency.* Guilford Press.

Booth, P. B., & Jernberg, A. M. (2010). *Theraplay: Helping parents and children build better relationships through attachment-based play.* Jossey-Bass.

Bowlby, J. (1982). *Attachment and loss: Vol. 1. Attachment* (2nd ed.). Basic Books. (Original work published 1969)

Bush, N. R., Sullivan, A. D. W., Norona-Zhou, A., et al. (2025). Early life stress effects on children's biology, behavior, and health: Evidence, mediators, moderators, and solutions. *Annual*

*Review of Psychology*. Advance online publication. https://doi.org/10.1146/annurev-psych-072225-121053

California Department of Health Care Services. (2022–2024). *CalAIM Enhanced Care Management and Community Supports guidance.*

Center for Health Care Strategies. (2023). *Coordinating Medicaid health-related social services through community care hubs.*Center for Systems Awareness. (n.d.). *Compassionate Systems Framework.*

Centers for Disease Control and Prevention. (2022–2024). *Adverse childhood experiences (ACEs) prevention resources.*

Centers for Disease Control and Prevention. (2023). *Maternal mortality and racial disparities in the United States.*

Centers for Medicare & Medicaid Services. (2023). *Coverage of health-related social needs (HRSN) services in Medicaid and CHIP* (State Health Official Letter).

Coates, T.-N. (2015). *Between the world and me.* Spiegel & Grau.

Collaborative for Academic, Social, and Emotional Learning. (2020). *CASEL framework for social and emotional learning.*

DeGruy, J. (2017). *Post traumatic slave syndrome: America's legacy of enduring injury and healing* (Revised ed.). Uptone Press.

Ferenczi, S. (1988). Confusion of tongues between adults and the child. In M. Balint & N. Jackson (Eds.), *Final contributions to the problems and methods of psychoanalysis* (pp. 156–167).

Karnac. (Original work published 1932) hooks, b. (2000). *All about love: New visions*. William Morrow.

Fields, N. T. (2026). *Play Now. Thrive Later. The Brain Well-Being Model® and Collective Care in Action®: A Framework for Healing Individuals, Families, and Communities*. Therapeutic Play Foundation.

Hughes, K., Bellis, M. A., Hardcastle, K. A., Sethi, D., Butchart, A., Mikton, C., Jones, L., & Dunne, M. P. (2017). The effect of multiple adverse childhood experiences on health: A systematic review and meta-analysis. *The Lancet Public Health, 2*(8), e356–e366.

JAMA Network Open. (2023). Racial disparities in mortality and health care outcomes in the United States. *JAMA Network Open.*

Kaiser Family Foundation. (2023). *Racial disparities in health outcomes and access to care.*

Landreth, G. L. (2012). *Play therapy: The art of the relationship* (3rd ed.). Routledge.

Los Angeles County Department of Public Health. (2023–2025). *State of Black Los Angeles County* (Reports and trend analyses).

Malchiodi, C. A. (2015). *Creative interventions with traumatized children*. Guilford Press.

McEwen, B. S. (1998). Protective and damaging effects of stress mediators. *New England Journal of Medicine, 338*(3), 171–179.

Menakem, R. (2017). *My grandmother's hands: Racialized trauma and the pathway to mending our hearts and bodies*. Central Recovery Press.

National Academies of Sciences, Engineering, and Medicine. (2019). *Integrating social care into the delivery of health care: Moving upstream to improve the nation's health*. National Academies Press.

National Scientific Council on the Developing Child. (2014). *Excessive stress disrupts the architecture of the developing brain: Working Paper 3* (Updated ed.). Center on the Developing Child at Harvard University.

Oaklander, V. (1988). *Windows to our children: A Gestalt therapy approach to children and adolescents*. Gestalt Journal Press.

Perry, B. D., & Szalavitz, M. (2006). *The boy who was raised as a dog: And other stories from a child psychiatrist's notebook*. Basic Books.

Porges, S. W. (2011). *The polyvagal theory: Neurophysiological foundations of emotions, attachment, communication, and self-regulation*. W. W. Norton.

Schore, A. N. (2003). *Affect dysregulation and disorders of the self*. W. W. Norton.

Senge, P., Hamilton, H., & Kania, J. (2015). The dawn of system leadership. *Stanford Social Innovation Review, 13*(1), 27–33.

Shonkoff, J. P., & Garner, A. S. (2012). The lifelong effects of early childhood adversity and toxic stress. *Pediatrics, 129*(1), e232–e246.

Substance Abuse and Mental Health Services Administration. (2020). *National guidelines for behavioral health crisis care: Best practice toolkit*.

Suzuki, W. (2021). *Good anxiety: Harnessing the power of the most misunderstood emotion.* Atria Books.

U.S. Surgeon General. (2021). *Protecting youth mental health: The U.S. Surgeon General's advisory.*

Van der Kolk, B. A. (2014). *The body keeps the score: Brain, mind, and body in the healing of trauma.* Viking.

World Health Organization. (2022). *World mental health report: Transforming mental health for all.*

Zero To Three. (2022–2024). *Infant and early childhood mental health resources.*

# Foundational Clinical and Cultural Lineage

The Brain Well-Being Model® and Collective Care in Action® emerge from an interdisciplinary lineage that spans clinical science, public health, and community-rooted healing traditions. This work is deeply informed by:

- Attachment science, which establishes safety in relationship as the foundation of regulation, identity, and exploration (Bowlby; Ainsworth).

- Polyvagal-informed neuroscience, which expands understanding of autonomic regulation, neuroception of safety and threat, and social engagement (Porges; Schore).

- Gestalt-based and relational play therapy, which center relationship, sensory awareness, and authentic expression in childhood healing (Oaklander; Landreth; Theraplay; ARC).

- Trauma neuroscience, toxic stress, and allostatic-load research documenting the biological impact of adversity and the conditions that support resilience and recovery across the life course (McEwen; Shonkoff; van der Kolk; National Scientific Council on the Developing Child).

- Public health, equity, and social-determinants scholarship identifying structural forces—racism, poverty, environmental harm, and policy design—as core drivers of mental and physical health outcomes (CDC; Harvard Center on the Developing Child; LA County ARDI and State of Black Los Angeles reports).

- Compassionate systems and organizational regulation frameworks, which treat institutions and leadership as nervous-system environments that can either amplify Guard Mode or support collective regulation and belonging (Center for Systems Awareness; Senge and colleagues).

- Black literary, theological, and cultural lineages that name trauma, survival, love, and collective care as intertwined realities (for example, Baldwin, Angelou, hooks, Coates, DeGruy, Menakem), alongside other global traditions of resistance and repair.

- Cultural and community healing practices carried by doulas, community health workers, promotoras, faith leaders, elders, artists, barbers and stylists, coaches, organizers, and relational caregivers whose everyday labor has long sustained nervous systems outside formal clinics.

Together, these streams form a living clinical and cultural inheritance in which relationship is intervention, the body is knowledge, play is regulation, community is medicine, and healing is understood as a collective, intergenerational task rather than an individual achievement.

The Brain Well-Being Model® does not replace these parent traditions. It integrates them into four simple domains of awareness, somatic, perceptual, relational, and aspirational, so that complex science can be used by families, youth, clinicians, educators, community health workers, faith leaders, and organizers in everyday life. Collective Care in Action® extends this lineage into environments, policies, and workforce design, translating decades of evidence and generations of community wisdom into practice pathways that can be seen, measured, and sustained across systems.

This text is offered as one contribution inside that broader lineage—an integration, not a replacement, for clinical, educational, public-health, spiritual, and community application across generations.

# About the Author

Nakeya T. Fields, LCSW, PPSC, Registered Play Therapist-Supervisor

Nakeya T. Fields is a clinician, play therapist, social worker, and founder of two community-based organizations in South Los Angeles: Therapeutic Play Foundation and Innovative Wellness Consulting. She is the creator of the Brain Well-Being Model®, the Brain Well-Being Index, and Collective Care in Action®—frameworks designed to translate neuroscience, trauma research, and attachment theory into practical tools for individuals, families, and communities.

Her work is rooted in the belief that healing is relational, embodied, and collective, and that communities have always practiced care long before systems gave it a name. Drawing from Gestalt-based play therapy, somatic practice, public-health equity movements, and Black literary and healing traditions, Nakeya has spent more than a decade designing spaces where nervous systems can move from survival toward thriving—through Resilience Studios™, ARTGard spaces, wellness labs, and community-driven programming.

She holds a Master of Social Work degree and has trained extensively in therapeutic play, trauma-informed care, and community health models. Her organizations have partnered with schools, managed-care plans, workforce development programs, and community-based agencies across Los Angeles County to bring the Brain Well-Being Model® into real-world practice.

As a Black woman raising a son in Los Angeles, Nakeya writes from lived experience as much as from clinical training. Her work is shaped by the question that threads through every chapter of this book:

*What would it mean to design the world our ancestors were denied, but our children deserve?*

She lives in Los Angeles with her son, Amare, and their two dogs, Nova and Oreo.

# Play Now. Thrive Later.